On a Clear Day

9/11 — An Eyewitness Account

[signature]

January 9, 2014

On a Clear Day
9/11 — An Eyewitness Account

Bert Upson

Thunderbird Press
P.O. Box 524
Rancho Mirage, CA 92270

On a Clear Day
9/11 – An Eyewitness Account
Bert Upson

Copyright ©2012 by Bert Upson

Published by
Thunderbird Press
P.O. Box 524
Rancho Mirage, CA 92270
www.thunderbirdpress.net

Title by Joan Upson
Cover Art and Illustrations by Doug Bunn
Book Design by Jean Denning
InDesign layout by Karoline Butler

Library of Congress Control Number: 2012945085

Upson, Bert
    On a Clear Day
    ISBN: 0-9860149-0-7 (paperback)
    ISBN: 0-9860149-1-5 (e-book)

Printed in the United States of America

This book is dedicated to those who were lost on 9/11
and to my wife, Joan, my children and grandchildren—
may they never live to see a day like this again

Acknowledgments

I would like to acknowledge the following people and organizations, without whose help this story would not be told:

My wife, **Joan Upson**, forever my inspiration and guiding light, who kept me on target and helped edit the story with a keen eye for accuracy.

Jean Denning, my inspirational, precise and relentless editor for detail and accuracy and my new friend and publisher. She made this possible. **Karoline Butler** for formatting the book and designing the cover. **Doug Bunn** for his remarkable drawings and cover art.

My first readers: Sabin Robbins and **Frank Peabody**, supporters and lifelong friends of seventy years, **Anne Curry, Michael Hemp, Don Hudson, Anne Smith, Dwight Townsend and Jan Wolfson**.

Bob Brink and **Seth Hoyt**, former clients at *Hearst Magazines* and fellow Yale classmates, who encouraged me and provided leads to stories for magazine publishers.

Dick McKinley, who got me started by encouraging me to write my autobiography. **John Annarino**, whose course on creative writing taught me the meaning of the word "terse." **Renee Espar**, whose course in writing an autobiography taught me the importance of being brutally honest with myself and the importance of establishing authenticity, as well as boosting my confidence in my writing ability. **My fellow classmates** in John's and Renee's writing courses who gave me constructive criticism and hope.

Carrie Ann of Carmel, California, for various story ideas and for her interest and encouragement. **Janet Asten**

of Rancho Mirage, California, for permission to print her poem *Prayer for September 11.* **Alison Bate and Dena Berger** who guided me and put me onto the story of the "Boatlifters" and encouraged me with my book. **Jessica Davis**, *Palm Desert Patch*, who set up my first internet interview after 9/11. **Katie Dodson**, owner of the Wildhorse Café in King City, California, for participating in my cover research. **John Doswell** of the Working Harbor Committee for permission to print the list of 9/11 rescue boats. **Laura Dudnick**, Editor of the *San Mateo Patch*, for helping me line up internet publicity channels. **Paul Fridlund,** co-owner of Pilgrim's Way Book Store of Carmel, California, for cover suggestions. **Sylvia Medina,** Editor-in-Chief, Rutgers Law Review for permission to print "A New Kind of War." **The Rancho Mirage (California) Library librarians** who helped me find reference material. **Bernice Bender, Anne Curry, Bob Doran, Don Hudson, David McCullough, the Carmel, California Fire Department and my Friends and Neighbors** for their interest, inspiration and encouragement.

PinArt who gave me permission to reprint their pin art, "September 11, 2001 — Never Forget."

All my sources for background material, especially **Wikipedia**, 9/11 Research, and *New York Magazine* who provided the bulk of my research.

Preface

On Tuesday, September 11, 2001, four suicide attacks were carried out against the United States of America. Nineteen terrorists belonging to al-Qaeda and masterminded by Osama bin Laden hijacked and flew into heavily populated buildings in New York City and the Washington, D.C., area.

Two of the passenger jets were deliberately flown into the twin towers of the World Trade Center in New York City, causing both towers to collapse. Actually, three towers collapsed, including Tower #7 which caught fire from the flying debris that had landed on top of it from the North and South Towers. A third passenger jet was flown into the Pentagon in Arlington, Virginia. A fourth passenger jet failed in its terrorist threat to the White House and crashed in a field in Shanksville, Pennsylvania, because brave passengers interceded in the evil mission and forced the plane to crash before it reached its target. Two of the flights had originated in Boston, one in Newark and one in Dulles International outside of Washington, D.C. The two flights that affected my life, which had originated at Logan International Airport in Boston, American #11 and United #175, were those destined to slam into the World Trade Center in New York where I would be working that day.

More than 3,000 people perished—256 passengers and crew were killed in the airplane crashes, including the 19 hijackers; 2,753 people died in the towers, including rescue workers—emergency medical technicians, firemen and policemen trying to free people from the upper floors.

There are some discrepancies in the body count depending on the source, but the above correlates with other statistics I have seen.

I was in the South Tower when the North Tower was hit—and escaped—mere minutes before United #175 would obliterate our conference room.

My story titled *On A Clear Day*, which you are about to read, is based on my personal experience.

Today there are many who still suffer mentally from post-traumatic stress and physically from inhalation damage—and others whose life spans have been threatened by cancer and related lung diseases.

I would be included in the post-traumatic shock statistics. I still have twinges of it whenever I dwell on that infamous day. I have occasional memory lapses about the sequence of events that afternoon. I also endured some temporary lung inflammation resulting from inhalation of pulverized steel, asbestos and heaven knows what else, all hazardous materials. I guess shell shock best describes my condition even ten years later, but I believe I think and behave normally, nor do I have a victim mentality. I am optimistic and have a positive view of the future. Nothing can take that away from me.

There are aspects of that day that don't seem to have been covered by the news media, including the boatlift of a half million frightened souls from the banks of the Hudson River and Battery Park. It was reputably the largest boatlift in the history of the world, yet it remained obscured until recently for reasons unknown.

Nor does it seem that the role of the rescue dogs received much attention in the press. Originally there were one hundred rescue dogs sent from all around the country. At this writing, only twelve have survived as far as I know. Generally unknown also was the use of robots to search spaces for bodies and body parts that were inaccessible to the rescuers.

I expect to acquaint you with some of the missing pieces as I tell my story, giving you a more complete picture of that remarkable day of infamy, including a timeline and summary of the 9/11 Commission Report.

My account cannot possibly cover all the happenings and ramifications of 9/11, nor the multitude of heroic actions by firemen, police, EMTs, as well as ordinary citizens who rose to the call. I give them profound thanks and solemnly promise them I will never forget them.

— Bert Upson
September 11, 2012

Contents

September 10, 2001

My Arrival in New York

After a routine early morning flight from San Francisco, I arrived at New York's JFK airport at around 5:30 P.M. on September 10, 2001. The following day, I was to conduct a training seminar for Vestek, one of my clients. The general manager of Vestek, Keith Webster, had the pull to arrange my stay at the Club Quarters, a small, private hotel not generally known to the public, located near Wall Street.

My dinner plan after checking into my hotel was to head for the top of the World Trade Center's North Tower's famous restaurant, "Windows on the World." I had not been there before.

Windows on the World was one of New York's finest restaurants. In addition to its reputation for superb dining, it was heralded for its commanding panoramic view of the east, south and west sectors of lower Manhattan, including the Hudson River plying its waters with magnificent cruise ships, the ubiquitous tug boats, beautiful private yachts and the Statue of Liberty.

My hotel made a dinner reservation for me, and after unpacking and freshening up, I headed north by foot to the World Trade Center, only eight blocks distant, and a fabulous dining experience. Christine Olender, the assistant general manager, greeted me, seated me by a south-facing window and presented me with a menu, the likes of which I had never seen before nor been able to afford. Christine must have sensed that I did not like to dine alone as she was extremely attentive to me, which I especially appreciated. The food lived up to its reputation. I finished dinner around nine P.M., said *au revoir* to Christine and the wait staff in my best French and left to return to the hotel. I would never see Windows or Christine again.

Returning to the hotel, I hit the sack with contentment and anticipation of the next day.

Meanwhile, in Boston, Massachusetts, a group of nine Muslim terrorists were celebrating what they knew would be their last supper as they made flight preparations for the next morning.

September 11, 2001

My Arrival at the World Trade Center

Early on the morning of Tuesday, September 11, 2001, after a scrumptious buffet breakfast, I left the comfort of the Club Quarters and leisurely walked the eight blocks to the World Trade Center to give my leadership development seminar.

The day had started with the weather clear as crystal, with a cloudless and cerulean blue sky, as beautiful as ever seen in New York City. The temperature was 84 degrees Fahrenheit.

Hurricane Erin was bearing down on New York City from the southeast. Shortly before the World Trade Center towers were hit, Erin turned away. If it had continued on its path and reached New York, the events of 9/11 could not have happened — at least, not that day. The clarity of the day was a real gift to the hijackers, making instrument flying unnecessary.

Apparently, the weather was perfect throughout the nation. In pilot jargon, a clear day like this is known as "severe clear." All the airports were open, and it was later reported that over four thousand planes were flying innocently to their destinations, including the not-so-innocent four planes harboring nineteen terrorists.

My seminar that day was to be one of my last. I was seventy years old and had worked for fifty years in advertising, sales and human resources development. My wife and I lived in Palm Desert, California, a perfect retirement location. I planned to retire soon after giving this last management development seminar to this group of fourteen executives at Vestek, a Thompson Financial subsidiary.

I knew most of the executives who would be attending my seminar from a previous engagement. They weren't exactly what you might call "friends," but I had spent enough time with most of them to feel our relationships were more than just cordial. We greeted each other warmly on a first-name basis, exchanging the usual pleasantries. I knew three of the executives pretty well: Keith Webster, Louis Calvin Williams III, and Bob Rasmussen. I would never see Lou and Bob again.

My seminar was scheduled to begin at 10:00 A.M. It was only 8:35 on that glorious, clear day. I had arrived early to learn more about the company's competitive situation and expectations of my services.

I entered #2 World Trade Center (the South Tower) from the east. The attendants at the desk were cheerful and polite and phoned up my arrival to Keith Webster, my contact. After being photographed, I donned my ID badge and headed for the elevators.

At 8:40 I arrived on the 78th floor, having taken the express elevator. I didn't know it at the time, but the 78th floor was destined to become a historic marker.

My subject for the day was "How to Invent Your Future and Reinvent Yourself." Everybody was waiting eagerly for me to start. So was I. Most had heard my similar presentation several years ago, and their sales had doubled in the meantime. My mission that day was to teach them how to set and implement even bigger goals to accelerate sales and reach the next level of perfection. That's my specialty, and having a receptive audience and a proven record boosted my confidence. Little did I, or they, know what the immediate future would bring.

In under thirty minutes — instead of "re-inventing yourself and inventing your future" — the theme would be more like "how to save yourself to live another day."

9

American 11 Hits the North Tower

Several of us were sipping our coffee and getting settled in the conference room, waiting for the rest of the group to arrive.

What happened next was so fast — like fast forwarding a tape — that I am unclear of the details. Suddenly there was a muffled **WHOOMPH** from the north side of the building. I could feel the air suck in . . . and our building tremble. The conference room seemed to sway. We found out later that the trembling we had felt had come from a powerful shock wave in the North Tower that had traveled down to the ground and back up again with such force that it shook our building across the street.

It felt like an earthquake, similar to several smaller ones I had experienced in Palm Desert where I live. In fact, it could have been considered an earthquake, but generated from the sky. Seismic signals from 9/11 were captured as though they came from an actual earthquake. On the Richter scale, the first impact of the North Tower, which I felt, registered a 0.9 magnitude. The actual collapse of the North Tower an hour or so later registered a 2.3 magnitude; the tremor was felt as far away as Maine.

In 1956, I had been a gunnery officer and forward observer at Ft. Sill, Oklahoma, exposed to the sounds of all sorts of weapons, large and small, including the atomic cannon. None of these weapons sounded like what we heard, but it was similar to a mortar being fired.

I had also been in the bombing of the Mobil Oil Building many years previously. What I heard then was nothing like that either. What I heard on 9/11 was unique to my ears and eerie, making the hairs stand up on my neck and giving me goose bumps just like in a scary movie.

Keith turned to me and said, "What the hell was that?"

"I don't know," I said, "but I'm going to take a look around." I ran down the hall in the direction of the sound but found no evidence of a bomb, or anything else that might have produced the sound and movement we experienced.

What was it? At worst, it could be the first strike of a nuclear attack. But, the more I thought about it, if it were a nuclear event, I wouldn't still be there — period. Could the explosion have come from the North Tower? It was such an unnerving sound and not traceable to anything on our floor as far as I could tell.

Finding nothing, I returned to the conference room and looked out the window. Towards the west, I noticed that the clear day of just a few minutes ago was gone. Now the sky was a darker grey, cluttered with what appeared to be confetti. I later learned it was shredded paper and pulverized concrete and gypsum flying by at an enormous speed — recorded at 75 mph. The prevailing wind was blowing most of the detritus out over Brooklyn where much of it ended up in people's backyards. The rest was floating over the streets abutting the Towers.

Trying to treat lightly and take the edge off what I believed to be a perilous situation, I asked those in the conference room with a trace of joviality in my voice, "Is there a parade in town? . . . How did they know I was here?" Someone remarked that if there were a parade, it would be unlikely that confetti would be thrown from the floors above — and, besides, the windows didn't open. Nor does confetti fly sideways at such velocity.

Uh-oh, I repeated to myself, *maybe it really is the beginning of a nuclear attack*, as I had first imagined, even the beginning of World War III. But then I reminded myself, if it were a nuclear attack, I wouldn't be feeling or thinking anything. I read somewhere that only cockroaches survive a nuclear attack. Not being a cockroach, my chances of survival would be nil.

A sense of urgency set in as we all seemed to reach different conclusions about the noise and the tremors in the building. I wasn't about to wait around for a consensus of opinion, but I didn't know the fastest way out. My next thought was, "Where are the stairs?"

Should I Stay or Go?

A little inner voice said "get out". . . call it intuition. I was unsure of the location of the nearest emergency exit, but one of the new women, I think her name was Carol, said she knew how to get to the express elevator. Keith was busy trying to get everyone out of the conference room, but some were reluctant to leave, not believing it was that serious.

A little before 9:00 A.M., Carol and I ran toward the emergency exit and elevator. At this point, there was mass confusion in the building. The stairwell was jammed, despite the lack of information of what was happening. People tend to run to the stairs in high rises in times of uncertainly and fear. The feeling of urgency quickly turned into panic. As we rounded a corner and spotted the elevator, we saw posted the usual sign noting, "IN CASE OF AN EMERGENCY, DON'T TAKE THE ELEVATOR. TAKE THE STAIRS." I was skeptical about going down 78 flights of stairs, possibly in the dark. Besides, following directions has never been my strong suit. You see, I am a bit of a maverick.

I don't claim to be a math expert, but I quickly calculated that even at thirty seconds per floor, it could take over forty minutes to force our way down seventy-eight flights of stairs, jostling with the hordes that were beginning to mass. Remembering my ordeal in the Mobil Oil Building bombing in 1977—walking down thirty-nine flights of stairs—which was minor compared to what I was now facing, helped fortify my decision.

We were just plain lucky . . . or blessed . . . or both. Timing is everything. So is location in a situation like this. If we had been in the North Tower when it was hit, we wouldn't have had options like this; depending on where one was, there might not have been an elevator or even stairs available for escape. People on the north side of the North Tower found that out, much to their horror.

My decision that the lesser risk and fastest way out was the elevator turned out to be the right decision. I found out later that one stairway, Stairway "B," where we were, was obliterated by the crash of United #175 shortly afterwards. Only Stairway "A" was operational, and it was on the opposite side of our floor. Of course, we didn't know that then. Even taking the elevator was risky—it could either crash or stop between floors if the electricity went off, as it did stop between the thirty-second and thirty-third floors on its next round trip.

An express elevator arrived within seconds after Carol and I got there. If it had not presented itself at that very moment, my decision might have changed, and I might have opted for the stairs. Seeing those doors open to let us on was a tremendous relief. Carol and I squeezed on. We were packed like proverbial sardines. We had to push the latecomers off or the elevator doors would not have been able to close. I felt bad about doing that. Not all of them would have made it out unharmed physically. I can still hear the ones we left behind pounding on the elevator doors and screaming, "let me on," "help me," "save me." I tried to shut them out of my mind. I am shuddering as I write this over ten years later. I have never said anything about this to anybody until now. My feelings of guilt have become embedded in my psyche.

This was the last round trip made by that elevator. It went back up to the 78th floor, and people got on expecting to go all the way down and to safety. But that did not happen. The elevator made it just past the 32nd floor when it stopped. The occupants had to climb out between floors and walk down the rest of the way lighted by only the emergency lights. At least they were below the impending impact of United #175 on the 78th floor.

In what passed as an eternity, Carol and I and perhaps thirty others on our elevator car landed at the mezzanine, and not too gently because of the overweight of our elevator car. It was probably more like a minute and a half trip. (Because the WTC buildings were so tall, the elevators were designed to travel at a rate of speed that moved from floor to floor in less than a second.) I think many of the occupants were holding their breaths and counting. I know I was. When the elevator door opened, the occupants spilled out onto the mezzanine where the elevator starters directed us to depart from the north exit to our right. Since we had been notified over the loudspeakers that it wasn't our building, the South Tower, that "was hit," but the North Tower, exiting right toward the North Tower didn't make sense to me. We were getting mixed messages. For the second time that day, the maverick in me saved me. We didn't obey, doing just the opposite of what we were told and, instead, proceeded left towards the southeast exit instead.

Many people stayed in the building and returned to their offices after being told, and I remember it word for word, "it wasn't our building that was hit, so it's safe to return to your offices, *as far as we know.*" From my communications training, knowing how some people listen, I suspected they were tuning out the part about, "as far as we know." They stayed put, including three of our associates. We hadn't even noticed their absence. It was a mad dash for the exits with every man for himself. Miraculously, Carol and I made it to an exit and found ourselves propelled onto the street.

United 175 Hits the South Tower

Still thinking this might be the first strike of a nuclear attack, Carol and I headed south and east toward the East River and Brooklyn, all the way across town. Outside the building, we felt safe. But were we? We didn't know what might happen next. A multitude of questions filled my thoughts: Was the attack over? What protection would the river be unless we could get across to Brooklyn? Would there be boats there waiting to ferry us across? How would we get back? Could we swim across? Would we make it over or be hit by a boat or become exhausted and drown? I had sailed on the East River before and remembered the tides were treacherous and the barges going with the tide plentiful. We didn't know of the massive boat rescue operation about to take place a short distance away.

Suddenly, my thoughts were interrupted by a monumental explosion. Carol and I turned around and looked up, spellbound. We saw what looked like the tail of a big plane going into our building about two-thirds of the way up in the vicinity of our conference room floor.

According to the official record, at 9:03:02, United Flight 175 crashed at about 590 mph into the south face of the South Tower between floors 77 and 85.

I calculated later that our escape between the moment we decided to run for it and the moment the United flight hit our conference area had provided only a few minutes' window. That's only minutes between instant death and living to see another day. Then I knew what luck—or fate—was.

Our floor had been obliterated. Anyone remaining in or around there would have been consumed by ignited jet fuel. Three of our original group who had been in the conference room turned out to be unaccounted for.

At the sound of the explosion and witnessing a spectacular fireball, Carol and I became even more frightened and picked up our pace, now dashing for our lives. In addition to the ash and soot coming our way from the north, there was an acrid odor in the air.

Our building would soon become a towering inferno and disappear from the face of the earth forever. I recalled later the movie "Towering Inferno," but this inferno was not of the Hollywood variety. It would not have a happy ending.

The crowd mentality became fiercer and fiercer. Everyone had one thing in mind: To save himself or herself, and to hell with anybody else. The mob was out of control and growing larger and larger every moment. I could feel people breathing down my neck. The fireball from the North Tower, enveloped in smoke, was in hot pursuit. We could feel the air getting hotter and hotter. I think the word "maelstrom" is a good word to describe the situation.

Carol got knocked down by a man tall enough to be a center for the New York Knicks. He didn't stop or even look back to see what he had done. Although I feared being trampled if I stopped for her, my first concern was for her life. I bent over to pick her up off the pavement, thereby preventing her from being trampled to death. Turning and glancing northward from whence we had come as I stooped to pick her up, I was overwhelmed by the two Towers belching like ancient dragons shooting fire and smoke only a few blocks distant. Shock and awe came to mind fleetingly as the sight spurred me on to greater efforts. I was lucky not to have been run over. Carol said I had saved her life. Perhaps I had. She had saved mine by getting us to the elevator and out of the building in one piece.

Finally accepting this was no nuclear attack, I aborted the idea of swimming across the East River. We were now in range of my hotel, the Club Quarters on William and Pine. Hiding out there seemed to make more sense than swimming for it.

I usually stayed at the Marriott in Tower Number 3, but when I tried to make a reservation, there were no vacancies. The Marriott was, of course, completely destroyed shortly after the South Tower fell. Part of the landing gear from the plane hitting the South Tower had landed on the roof, causing it to start fires that consumed the building.

Was it a coincidence I wasn't staying at the Marriott this time, because my natural instinct would have been to return there and use the underground tunnel to get out instead of going up to the street level. Was this luck or divine intervention?

We did not know it at the time, but luckily, the subways on the east side were still operational, which offered an option for later. The Lexington Avenue line would prove to be the best way for me to get to midtown and safety.

Pandemonium Reigns

The crowd continued to swell and press on with greater and greater intensity as Carol and I broke into a mad dash. Although I could run faster than she, I slowed and held her hand so she wouldn't be left behind, lessening her risk of being knocked down again. There was utter pandemonium on the street, with people screaming and running for their lives. The stampede was now in full force.

Behind us, people were jumping out of windows from the uppermost floors of Tower #1, the North Tower. For others who had hoped for a helicopter rescue from the roof, apparently the door to the roof was locked. Even if they had made it to the roof, and the trap doors were open, the roof would have been incredibly hot, impossible to walk on—and the area was not large enough for a big helicopter to land—so they stayed or jumped. One jumper hit and killed a rescue worker on the street. Stay and be burned to death, or jump . . . that's what they had to be thinking. Not much of a choice, is it? We were horrified at the prospect.

After a while, the noise from the screaming crowd began to subside. I think people running were conserving their energy, or perhaps they sensed they were out of imminent danger. Or maybe they were exhausted.

I can remember a sense of being in a surreal world where I was running at the front edge of celluloid film struggling to keep ahead of the cloud of dust bearing down on me. I was running as fast as I could, but the ball of fire and smoke was gaining ground. I would be consumed and die before the film ran out. My imagination was hyperactive that day.

Temporary Refuge

At 9:16 A.M., Carol and I arrived, breathless, at the Club Quarters Hotel. Once inside, I stationed Carol in the stairwell between the dining room and lobby away from the windows. In Palm Desert, California, that's what we were trained to do in the event of an earthquake. This wasn't an earthquake, but I thought putting her there provided some safety if the building got hit since I knew of no alternative.

After securing Carol, I went into the dining room to be sure the burners under the warming pans were turned off and then into the kitchen to locate fire extinguishers. I had no business doing this, but the hotel manager noticed what I was doing and didn't interfere with my safety concerns.

The kitchen help must have thought I was a new manager. They did what I asked. I don't know why I took over, but no one else seemed to be in charge. I simply stepped up to the plate. They had been watching the unfolding drama live on TV. They were as frightened as we who had escaped. They actually knew more than we did, because we weren't watching the action on TV — we were in the midst of it.

The hotel manager saw that the dining room was under control and asked me to close the bar for her. The remaining drinkers were Australians. If you have ever tried to separate an Aussie from his Foster, I don't recommend it. Surprisingly and fortunately for me, with little persuasion, they grudgingly left the bar, but not without their Fosters.

As I was capping and storing the liquor, I saved a glass of vodka out for myself, thinking I might need it in case of an emergency. As a recovering alcoholic, it had been many years since I had had a drink, but it certainly was tempting this day.

Realizing it was safe to abandon the stairwell, Carol joined me at the bar, where we both watched CNN until we couldn't take it anymore. It was incredible. I still wasn't fully aware that I had been in the midst of such a catastrophe. It was like watching repeats of a B-western. I must have been in dreamland, not yet able consciously to acknowledge the frightening situation I was in. For a moment, I thought I was dreaming and had awakened, overwhelmed first by disbelief and then anguish and anger.

Wasn't this just a bad dream? I sure hoped so.

The hotel opened its doors to all comers, even if they were not registered guests. People of all descriptions came streaming in through the revolving door from the street, some crying and some coughing, smoke and ash accompanying them.

I organized a group of hotel residents to hand out dampened towels so people could remove the ash and soot from their faces. Every time that revolving door turned, I cringed. The room was filling with more smoke and more people as the doors revolved.

As I helped one lady wipe the ash and soot off her face, I was totally surprised to see she was a black woman. I remarked, "Oh, my God, you're black!"

She looked at me, chuckled and said, "Why not?" Then we laughed together. That was the first and only comic relief I had felt in the unfolding drama.

Fifteen minutes later with everything secure in the kitchen, dining room and bar, I headed up to my room on the 15th floor. Carol stayed downstairs with the rest of the group, all of whom were fixated on CNN.

The minute I got into my hotel room I placed a telephone call to my wife, Joan, who was in Portola Valley, California, visiting Mary McCann, her former roommate from Stanford University. This was about 6:30 A.M.

California time, earlier than Joan usually wakes up, but I knew Mary would be up and at work in the kitchen. Mary had always tuned in to CNN the moment she emerged from the bedroom, but hadn't yet done so this particular morning. I was surprised she had not heard of the attack on the Twin Towers. I told her to turn on the news because I had just escaped from the South Tower physically unscathed, and I wanted to tell Joan I had escaped and had returned safely to the hotel. Mary thought I was joking until I repeated myself three times. She finally turned on the TV and got all choked up as I relayed my recent flirtation with death. She then asked if she should wake up Joan to have me tell her in person. I always tell Joan in advance where I am staying, but she didn't know my seminar was going to be in the World Trade Center.

I said, "No, I don't want to disturb her. Just tell her I'm okay and will call her later." Thinking about it now, I can't understand why I said that, but I was probably in shock and wasn't thinking straight.

Neither Joan nor I had a cell phone yet, so we were dependent on land lines. I remembered she had a beauty parlor appointment that day, and I decided I would try to reach her there. When I called several hours later, Florence, her hairdresser, advised me, "She left, and you just missed her." Florence was shocked when I told her why I was calling. Now I really was feeling bad and guilty for not having Mary wake Joan that morning. I knew she would be worried about me.

That got me thinking about what she might do if I died. Had I planned adequately for her in the case of my death? Would she be taken care of financially? Would there be enough money? Who would take care of her if she needed help? Would she be able to travel as we loved to do together? Would there be another man? Could there be? I cringed at this thought, but then most of the men older than she would be gone anyway. Now that I am ten years older, nearly eighty, I still have those same thoughts. I wonder if other husbands have them, too.

Finally, I did get in touch with Joan back at Mary's, and she was relieved to hear my voice and be reassured that I was safe. In telling her they would probably be evacuating the hotels in the area, she gave me suggestions of people I could call and ask for a bed, which I appreciated. We rang off, and I went downstairs to see what was new.

Finding nothing new happening downstairs, I returned to my room. Shortly after, there was a knock on my door. I wondered who it could possibly be. Cautiously I slid the chain lock on and opened the door slightly. It was Carol. She looked beat. She just wanted to rest and get away from the din downstairs for a while.

I went downstairs just as a female police officer arrived and distributed surgical face masks. I was astonished by the unexpected response of the NYPD to our plight. How did they even know we were there? They were busy saving lives and closing down the area to keep the curiosity seekers, looters, and ambulance chasers out. To think of the survivors who were apparently out of harm's way went beyond the call of duty to my mind, or — was there something else coming we didn't know about? As I went outside later into the smoke, I realized how fortuitous her visit was. It was hard for me to breathe even wearing a mask.

Here I was stranded in a downtown hotel with around fifty people I didn't know wearing surgical masks and glued to the TV set in an atmosphere of gloom and doom. We probably looked like a bunch of Emperor penguins except we weren't on parade like the penguins in the television travelogues.

Stranded

By 9:30 A.M. on 9/11, all the bridges and tunnels into Manhattan had been closed. The FAA had already shut down the airspace throughout the country earlier at 9:17 A.M. We were told not to leave the hotel until an "all clear" was issued. There never was an "all clear." We were quarantined like the plague with no outside communication except what we could get from CNN coverage, which was incredibly good. We had nowhere to go and no way to get there.

The streets were jammed with police and emergency vehicles. No civilian traffic was permitted. There was no way out and no way in except by foot, and even then, the police had barricades to keep people out of what is now known as "ground zero." The noise of sirens and Klaxons was daunting. The odor was overpowering and noxious, making breathing arduous. I had smelled burning rubber before, but this was worse—more acrid and a little bit like barbecued meat. It turned out to be people burning in the upper floors of the buildings.

I said earlier that I wasn't prone to taking instructions, so I broke the curfew and went up to the corner and over to Greenwich Avenue which led directly to the towers. There was so much smoke that I couldn't see very far, nor could I be seen by the police. I was able to look far enough north, but didn't see anything where our building had stood. The South Tower wasn't there any more. Where had it gone, all 110 floors of it?

I then drifted over farther west to West Side Drive and down to the Battery where I got a view of what appeared to be a massive exodus of New Yorkers by rescue boats on the water. Hordes of people were lined up on the water's edge patiently waiting to be picked up by ferries, Coast Guard cutters, and tugboats.

Returning eventually to the haven of the Club Quarters, I realized how fortunate Carol and I were in following our intuition to run for it. I shuddered to think of the fate of all those remaining behind or trapped inside, especially those whom I had known.

The Wall Street area was now completely locked down, but a few straggling escapees covered with ash and soot were still on the go.

I stepped out again and ushered those who were willing into the refuge of the hotel. We were their Noah's Ark, and they were grateful. The police told me to get the hell inside.

Back inside the hotel, I asked the cook how we were going to feed all these people. I knew the kitchens in New York relied on morning resupply of food by truck since they have limited refrigerator storage capability. But today the trucks couldn't get in. No trucks; no food.

By this time, we had perhaps fifty people to feed. The chef, Frenchie, who was missing most of his uppers, looked at me and said, "That easy. We order out Chinese. What's your favorite?"

"Barbecue spare ribs," I answered without hesitation, finding it very hard to believe Frenchie could pull this off. How the Chinese got through to us I don't know, but they did. They brought shrimp, dumplings, sweet and sour pork, beef and broccoli and loads of Chinese chicken salad—and some extra barbecue spare ribs just for me in honor of my newly-attained celebrity status. It was a welcome treat. I must have been hungry but wasn't thinking about eating.

Rarely had the kitchen served more than a dozen or more guests for lunch because this was a small, private hotel and not well known for its food. We now had maybe fifty starving, emotionally upset souls, many of whom did not know where their family members or associates were. They had been waiting like expectant fathers outside the delivery room to hear the news.

Since I had been the one to extinguish the Sterno burners earlier that morning, I took it upon myself to replace them with new ones and ignite them to keep the food warm.

We set up a buffet. Everybody was orderly and especially polite, although the mood of the diners was somber. Most were waiting to hear from their "no show" relatives and friends. Everyone's eyes were glued to the giant TV over the bar in the dining room, where the events of the morning were repeated over and over with new material added. I must have seen the imploding Towers' visuals repeated at least twenty or thirty times during lunch—not much of an appetite inducement.

While Carol and I were having lunch, my friend and colleague, Keith Webster, called on Carol's cell phone to tell us he was safe. He had escaped northward from the South Tower. Luckily, he was able to get on one of the last subway trains to leave the station under the Towers, ending up in Chinatown. There was no way for us to rendezvous until the next afternoon at the memorial service for our three colleagues who still were unaccounted for.

After lunch, many of the diners thanked me personally as I proceeded to extinguish burners under the chafing dishes as I had earlier that day. This time there was no rush.

Carol decided to leave the hotel and try to retrieve her car further over on the Westside, and I retreated to my room. I shut off the air conditioner to keep the smoke out, partially filled the tub with cold water, soaked a bath towel, and put it under the door just as you are supposed to do in case of fire. This was instinctive behavior on my part because this wasn't a hotel fire.

I turned on the TV one more time, sat down at the desk, stared at the still full glass of vodka and started sending emails to my friends and family. After that, I began researching the internet for confirmation from the Constitution of the United States and the Bill of Rights, looking for a provision that says, "It is the duty of the federal government to protect its citizens from foreign invasion." I wanted to fix the blame. I was angry.

After mulling over what went wrong and getting nowhere about who was responsible, I decided to open the door of my hotel room and look down the hall, thinking how quiet it was and how strange it seemed to be held hostage in my own country by a man 10,000 miles away. By then, Osama bin Laden had been singled out as authorizing the attacks. It was now around 3:30 P.M.

Lockdown

After finishing my research on the computer and watching the tragic events unfold on CNN, I decided to check outside my room. Opening my hotel door, I saw the hall was filling with smoke emanating from the elevators and air vents. I realized that the recommended methods of surviving a hotel fire were not appropriate. It was time to retreat.

Before I did that, I thought I'd better try to find another place to stay. I followed my wife's advice and started calling around for a room that might be available.

First, I called my older brother, Stuart. He didn't know I was in New York and was shocked to hear of my plight. He had a lovely two-bedroom apartment in United Nations Plaza on 44th and First Avenue, overlooking the United Nations building and the East River, a perfect spot to rest after a harrowing day. He apologized, but he had no place for me to sleep that night. He was entertaining overnight clients, and all his extra beds and sofas were already spoken for. I was disappointed, as at that time I had no place to go. Weariness began to set in.

I then called several other people Joan had suggested. One, LuAnn Kip, my wife's former associate in the executive recruiting business, could fit me in with four other women who were also seeking refuge. That sounded tempting, but she was on the upper West Side where I preferred not to be.

Finally, after trying three more of Joan's suggestions with no success, I called the Helmsley Middletowne Hotel on 48th between Lexington and Third, where I had been a frequent and valued guest. They said they were filled up but they might have a room available if I would call back later. But I couldn't call back because there were no telephones available outside on the streets or on the subway, and I didn't own a cell phone. I knew I would have to leave the hotel. I was tired and discouraged with the lack of suitable lodgings, tired of calling around and ready to get moving after being cooped up all day.

I packed my overnight bag and put in a small flashlight, pocket knife and a package of peanut butter and cheese crackers in my pocket and headed for the stairs, leaving my computer and big suitcase behind. The hotel graciously offered to pick them up from my room and ship them to me in California.

Out the door I went, saying goodbye to room 1510. I wasn't chancing getting stranded on an elevator. The smoke in the hallway was dense. It had come in through the revolving doors downstairs and found its way up through the elevators and stairwells. My room was clear because I had had the sense to close the air conditioning vent to the outside to keep out the foul air and put a wet towel at the base of the door.

Not wanting to take the elevator, I headed for the emergency exit feeling my way down the hall and counting my steps. This is a practice I always follow when I am traveling. It was important to know how to get out of the hotel if the lights go out. Now I have added the condition of staying no higher than the fourth floor, which is as high as most fire ladders go.

Shortly after I got to the lobby, they told us the water was being shut off, and an hour later, they were going to turn off the electricity, as well. They passed out flashlights to everyone remaining in the hotel. This was a lockdown. We weren't survivors any more. We had become refugees. The order from the police to evacuate never came. They must have been too busy elsewhere. But the hotel decided that with no water and no electricity, it would be dangerous for us to stay. They would be unable to provide any services.

I don't know where all the hotel guests went, but being on the west side of New York near the Hudson River, the natural inclination would have been to head for the Battery where the Staten Island ferries docked. There they could be rescued and taken to Brooklyn, New Jersey or Staten Island by boat as I later discovered happened.

Around 4:30, still in shock and somewhat disoriented, I took off down the street to the east alone, heading for the Battery about two miles distant to grab the Lexington Avenue Subway, which I hoped was still operating north to 53rd and Third. This time period is a bit fuzzy in my mind. It took a really long time—at least three hours—for me to reach Battery Park across the tip of Manhattan, which is far more time than it should have taken. I can't remember why it took me so long, and can only guess I may have made some stops and/or walked in circles because of my confused state of mind.

Although it was still daylight, the streets were shrouded in darkness by the soot and smoke. It reminded me of the blizzard in New York many years ago where I had also been stranded. The flashlight the police had given me at the hotel came in handy in reading the street signs.

A well-armed policeman in S.W.A.T. gear (assault rifle and night-vision optics) materialized from nowhere. Blocking my way, he told me not to continue east but to detour south for the subway. I told him I was a tired old man with a heart problem and needed to continue the shortest distance east to the Lexington Avenue Subway. He said, "Look, buddy, I don't have time for all of this. I have other things to do." I looked at him again with his armament and decided not to challenge his wisdom. So we parted on good terms — but I was to see him again.

On my way once more, all of a sudden three seemingly innocent, tall teenaged boys approached me and blocked my way. As they neared, I saw that they weren't all that innocent. They asked where I had come from. I responded by asking them where they had come from. Their answer was, "From Brooklyn . . . we came to check things out." When I told them I had been in the World Trade Center, they said I was a hero (which I thought was a strange thing to say) and started shaking my hand. They wanted my autograph. I told them I would be glad to give it to them, but I didn't have a pen on me. Neither did they. I told them the last time someone had asked for my autograph she had mistaken me for John Chancellor, a well-known newscaster in the 1960s.

When they said they knew who John Chancellor was, I became suspicious. He had died many years before they were even apples in anyone's eyes. They asked if I had any money on me. I said, "No, I left it in the hotel," and started to walk away. Just as they made an attempt to mug me, the same S.W.A.T. policeman materialized again, thank God. The boys took off in a hurry. The policeman told me they were not from Brooklyn but members of a gang on the lower East Side out to mug pedestrians like me. I thanked him and continued on my way toward the Battery and subway. It seemed to me this was another close escape.

Were there going to be any more close calls? I asked myself. God, I hoped not.

I had to relieve my bladder and didn't want to do it in the street, despite the fact the streets were empty and no one would see me. I was afraid I might be caught and sent to jail for indecent public exposure. How would I explain that to my wife and friends? I could see the news article in my mind: "Bert Upson, aged 70, was apprehended for urinating on a public street and escorted to the 1st precinct house." Down the street I spotted a church yard and thought that might be as good a watering spot as any. Observing it was surrounded by a spiked fence at just about the level of my crotch, I decided it would be ill-advised to try to jump the fence risking being impaled on the spikes.

I continued on, confused, but hoping I was headed in the right direction to the subway station. Walking alone in the gloom and hazy afterglow of the burning towers on the darkening streets of Lower Manhattan can be a little scary, especially when people emerge mysteriously through the haze from nowhere. I had visions of Jack the Ripper careening down the cobble-stoned streets in a carriage. My imagination that evening was fearsome.

A little further on, I sighted a blinking neon sign that said, "BAR." On closer inspection I noted it was called "The Cracker Jack." In Chicago there was a men's gay bar by the same name. I wondered if they were cousins. I went down the steps, ordered a tonic and lime and headed to the men's room. All heads turned in my direction. This was obviously a neighborhood bar where newcomers are carefully checked out. I locked myself in the men's room and did my thing. When I returned to the bar, an attractive, young couple approached me and asked where I had come from. I told them. After we talked for a while, they kindly asked if I had a place to stay for the night because if not, they lived nearby and had a sofa bed I was welcome to use. I thanked them saying that I had made other plans, which was a little bit of a fairy tale, but something didn't feel right about being asked by a couple I had never met to stay with them. Besides that, I didn't want to be indebted to anyone. My intuition had served me well so far, and I decided to put my trust in it again. Thanking them and getting directions to the subway, I left the bar.

Sanctuary, at Last

After I left the bar, I made it to the subway just in time, thinking I would head for the Helmsley Middletowne Hotel to see if a room had become available. Fortunately, the East Side subway was still functioning. This was to be its last run of the day, just like my South Tower elevator. Eerily, I found myself alone on the subway. This was surreal, but, then, so had been the whole day.

I was beginning to feel secure until we stopped at 14th Street. There three more teenage boys got on and looked over at me. I thought, *Oh no, here we go again.* But luckily, nothing happened. My rumpled and dusty appearance may have put them off.

As the subway rattled northward underneath Lexington Avenue, every time it stopped to pick up the few passengers who had ventured out into the street possibly on their way to work, I did a double take as paranoia grabbed me. I remembered the threatening teenage hoodlums who had impeded my way earlier and was afraid that they or their cronies might get aboard and threaten me. I prayed this wouldn't happen. The Grand Central stop coming up next was usually the most populous station along the tracks, and I breathed more confidently as we stopped and started again before heading to my stop, 53rd and Third Avenue. No one of any significance got on. I exited at 53rd Street and Third Avenue and walked the five blocks to the Helmsley Middletowne Hotel. The Middletowne had been my home away from home for over twenty years. Leona Helmsley endeared herself to senior citizens by giving them a thirty percent discount on the rooms.

Lily Martinez, the assistant manager, whom I had known personally for years, came around the front desk and greeted me with a big hug. She could tell by the way I looked that I had been in a bad place and showed genuine concern over my welfare. She said she hardly recognized me.

Lily said, "I'm sorry, Mr. Upson, we couldn't hold your room because you didn't call back." Now I was stuck. Then she cracked a grin and added, "We may not have a room for you, but we do have a suite which is yours for the night—complimentary." I was overwhelmed with relief and gratitude.

I went upstairs to my suite and called Joan with my usual away-from-home "goodnight," told her where I was and about my day (but not about the muggers), and asked her to go to an ATM and use our debit cards to withdraw the maximum amount of cash from all our accounts and fill the gas tank. My fear was that there would be a run on the banks the next day and that there would be severe gasoline shortages just as there were in the oil shortages of 1974.

After calling Joan, I called my brother to tell him I had arrived safely at the Middletowne and was able to get their last room . . . a slight stretch. He sounded relieved and said he would come over to the hotel the following morning to see me.

By then it was well past my dinnertime. The Chiam Restaurant was next door. I was a frequent diner there and loved the food and fast service. Henry Leung, the owner and maître d', whom I had known for years, greeted me at the door, saw my condition and asked where I had been. I knew it was late and asked him when they closed. Henry replied, "Bert, we are open as long as you are here."

As I was waiting for my meal to arrive, I recalled an earlier amusing incident involving Henry. I wanted to be able to thank Henry in Chinese, so I asked the waiter, whom I had also known for years, how to say, "Thank you very much for your kind hospitality." The waiter told me. I tried to write it down phonetically in English as best as I could. After my meal I proudly repeated it to Henry. Henry looked shocked. He said, "Bert, do you know what you just said to me?"

"Yes, I'm saying thank you."

"No, you said you die a thousand deaths."

Now I was mortified and tried to apologize. I noticed the waiter laughing, and then Henry laughed, too. I realized it was a put-up job. Henry told me I needed to brush up on my Chinese! Henry put his arm around me when we parted and smiled. We were now bonded.

I reminded Henry of this incident, and we both had a good laugh.

After my Chinese feast, I went back to the Middletowne, watched the late night news to see if there were any new terrorist attacks and then went to bed. I thanked God for saving my life that day and leading me to safety, and then recited the 23rd Psalm, "The Lord is my Shepherd, I shall not want . . ." and added a prayer I remembered from my childhood, "Now I lay me down to sleep. I pray the Lord my soul to keep. If I should die before I wake, I pray the Lord my soul to take."

How would I know if I would wake up in the morning? I was lucky to be alive and unharmed physically, but I felt out of sorts.

September 12–14, 2001

A Welcome Visitor

But I *did* wake up in the morning of September 12th, completely disoriented and wondering where the hell I was. I don't ever recall waking up so angry.

Where had our government been the day before? Had the government been asleep? It seemed so. They run the country's defense, not me. They were not prepared for the unexpected. That's no excuse as far as I was concerned. There was time for them to have stopped at least one of the planes, but as I understand it, a recent change in protocol required the air command to get approval from the Secretary of Defense before empowering the interceptors to either escort a plane out of harm's way or shoot it down.

After showering and getting dressed, I stepped across 53rd Street to a coffee shop to get a Danish and cup of coffee. I thought it was to be just another day until looking up and seeing a mantle, which according to satellite imagery was a smoke plume covering Manhattan Island entirely. Wow! I took my Danish and coffee back to my room and turned on the TV to get caught up on the latest developments.

About twenty minutes later, there was a knock on the door. It was my brother, Stuart, coming to see how I was doing. He said he felt bad that he couldn't put me up the night before. I forgave him. This was the brother I had cherished all my life to the extent that I had tried to model my life after him. How could I be mad at him?

Stuart had saved me many times from the wrath of my father and helped me get into the advertising business, coming to my rescue when I got into trouble. He was chairman and CEO of Saatchi & Saatchi U.S., responsible then for the Toyota account. After Stuart retired at about age eighty, he received the highest award in advertising — election to the Advertising Hall of Fame. I even had followed him into Yale where he had been a tenor in the Yale Whiffenpoofs, as was I ten years later. He and his wife, Barbara, were always there when I needed them. One Christmas after my eldest son died in an automobile accident when he was seventeen, I was standing in the grand hall of the Pan Am Building admiring the beautiful tree surrounded by presents for inner city kids. I was not in a happy frame of mind. Standing there feeling sad and lonely, I felt an arm go around my arm and a voice saying, "How are you?" It was my brother, Stuart, who appeared out of nowhere. This was a remarkable coincidence, or maybe it was meant to be. He had lifted my spirits.

Now, here we were thirty-four years later, and he's in my hotel room asking, "Brother, how are you? Do you need anything?" Did you bring enough money to last until you can get out of here?" I told him fifty bucks would help, and he handed me five one-hundred dollar bills. I really didn't need the money, but I thought it might make him feel better about the night before.

The Yale Club Library

After Stuart left, and still upset and angry at our government, I took the bus to the Yale Club Library at 44th and Vanderbilt and spent the rest of the morning there continuing my research of the Constitution and Bill of Rights, as well as FBI and CIA mission statements and Secret Service agents' job descriptions. There must be something in one of them that fixes the blame for a tragedy like this. Whose fault was it? I wanted to know. This was my new mission, to find out. I had suspected it was the CIA's, but I had nothing to confirm or deny this until many years later. Knowing where the letdown in responsibility lay remained in the back of my mind.

Until learning more, I could only point the finger at George W. Bush. After all, he was President and Commander-in-Chief who is responsible for protecting us. Former President Truman made it clear when he put the sign on his desk in the oval office, "The buck stops here." It wasn't quite the same as seeing it in the Constitution or in the Bill of Rights, but good enough to answer my question of who is ultimately responsible.

[In a news conference on December 19, 2005, President Bush confirmed this saying ". . . as President and Commander in Chief, I have the constitutional responsibility and the constitutional authority to protect our country. Article II of the Constitution gives me that responsibility and the authority necessary to fulfill it."]

I went on to check FBI and CIA documents on the computer to ascertain their missions and roles in national defense. The closest I could come was the CIA, which was supposed to gather and analyze any and all information that could indicate a potential attack. Later on, I discovered that there had been many substantive warnings that there would be an attack on big buildings in the U.S. by al-Qaeda operatives that went unheeded by our leaders. Donald Rumsfeld, then Secretary of Defense, had even alluded to the possibility of an attack on American buildings in a staff meeting on the morning of 9/11 in the Pentagon.

Although the FAA did what I thought was a credible job in preparing to release the F-15s, when the attack planes were changing their courses, the transponders were disabled; and despite the clear skies, it would have been potentially disastrous to send the F-15s into a sky filled with domestic flights. The FAA failed in its mission to scramble the interceptors fast enough, which could have brought down at least one of the planes attacking the Pentagon and the plane which ultimately crashed in Pennsylvania. But who was responsible to give them the order? I believe the order to stand by and arm the planes came from one authority, the order to intercept came from another source and the order to fire came from a third party. It is confusing from the various sources I have examined. No one really had a handle on it, because an attack by our own planes had never been considered as a possibility.

The 9/11 Commission Report issued in 2004 stated that it was not the Commission's job to single out any single person or group as guilty of omission and therefore dereliction of duty. That was certainly convenient and politically correct, but I believe anyone causing a failure in our communications system prior to the attack should be held accountable, including those who may have doctored their timelines past facts to make it appear they reacted sooner than they did.

I asked then, and I ask again now, "Was there a cover-up?" Probably not. Just confusion fueled by fear and panic. Many of our top leaders were either out of the country or not in the capitol building at the time. The possibilities of a coordinated effort were limited for that reason and because the telephone communications were faulty, causing conversations to often break up. There was no game plan to prevent or intercept the hijackers of a domestic airplane. Our main line of defense had been SAC, a post-WWII relic aimed at shooting down Russian missiles. Not expecting an attack by domestic aircraft, our response to 9/11 was disorganized and outdated, geared as it was to an attack from Russia, rather than terrorists on our own soil. Condoleezza Rice remarked that she couldn't imagine an attack by foreign nationals who hijacked and even flew our planes. Apparently the lessons learned from the sneak attack on Pearl Harbor had gone unheeded by our security planners.

My analysis from reading all the public documentation available—that's hundreds of pages of testimony and news reporting during and after the event—is that there was a complete disconnect in communications among the government agencies, compounded by erratic phone service. Even President Bush remarked after returning to the White House on Air Force One that "the telephones on that plane were antiquated."

Feeling frustrated and no less angry, I left the library and returned to the hotel and checked out. A limousine had been sent by Vestek to pick me up to attend a memorial service for the three colleagues who had not left the building on 9/11 – and then take me to New Jersey, because I had agreed to conduct another leadership program before returning home.

Another Commitment

The airports were reopening the following day, but it was necessary for me to remain on the East Coast.

Before leaving California for the assignment in New York on 9/11, my long-term client, ADP, had asked me to do a two-day leadership development program for two of its top executives in New Jersey.

After the memorial service for our three dead associates, the limo took me to the Embassy Suites in Parsippany, New Jersey, where the ADP leadership program was to be held. I arrived late in the afternoon and after checking in, I retreated to my room to call home. Returning to the lobby a few minutes later, I was overjoyed to see a large bouquet of flowers on a stand near the entrance with my name inscribed on a plaque with the words, "We are grateful to have you with us — We'll never forget."

Under the circumstances of my recent harrowing experience in the South Tower, I could have asked for a postponement of the ADP gig and returned to my wife in California. That would have been the sensible thing to do. However, I felt committed to help these two people who were at risk of losing out on a promotion if they didn't learn how to improve their interpersonal relationships and understanding of team cooperation.

I felt duty bound. I wasn't going to let the evil machinations of one man, bin Laden, cause me to shirk my business obligations. Screw him. My wife and I talked it over, and she brought up the point that I would need to return to New York in a week or so which would mean another long and strenuous trip. So I stayed for two more days, but I paced myself by starting each seminar later in the morning and ending earlier than normal in the afternoon to conserve my mental and physical powers.

The ADP job went well, and I think I gained new respect from my client for staying and putting them ahead of my personal comfort. Besides, the suite was comfortable and the food excellent. I didn't mind being pampered for another day or two after my recent ordeal.

Recuperation

On the Road to Recovery

I returned to San Francisco on Saturday, September 15. My wife picked me up at the airport and drove me to Bodega Bay on the coast where we were house-sitting. The house was on a hill overlooking a golf course and the bay. It was near the beach, which elicited fond memories of our honeymoon in Hawaii in 1985.

At Bodega Bay I recuperated, or at least tried my best. It was difficult, and I was consumed by flashbacks to that horror-ridden day. There were restless nights and nightmares. In one nightmare, I dreamed bin Laden and his henchmen had invaded the beach below our house. In my dream, I had grabbed a couple of automatic rifles and a bandoleer of bullets, had run outside and destroyed his force, saving bin Laden for last. I shot him in the face. I became the John Wayne of Bodega Bay. He was my idol growing up (I could even imitate his swagger) as he saved our country from the Japanese in the Pacific Theatre. I was now protecting the country from bin Laden and al-Qaeda in the United States.

Since arriving in Bodega Bay, I developed what I feared was an abnormal pattern: At ten o'clock in the morning after breakfast, I would go downstairs to the living room overlooking the Pacific Ocean, light a fire in the over-sized stone fireplace, sit in an overstuffed easy chair and try to read, but would fall asleep for a couple of hours in front of the roaring fire. That was uncharacteristic of my morning routine, as I'm usually up and out of bed like a shot and could do more work in the morning than most people did all day.

But something was wrong. After a few days, my lungs started to bother me, probably from the toxic residue I had breathed in from the ash and soot of 9/11. At the Petaluma Hospital Emergency Room, the doctor who examined me exclaimed he had been the attending physician during the construction of the South Tower. What a coincidence. Or, was it?

I seemed to be lazy all day long and sort of acted like a zombie. I didn't know it at the time, but this behavior is symptomatic of depression and post-traumatic stress. Then, I drifted into denial that this could be happening to me—a good family man, successful advertising executive and accomplished entrepreneur!

One incident that snapped me out of my lassitude and lethargy was that of an airplane from the north that kept flying over the Bodega Bay house, then circled and disappeared from sight. Then back it would come and repeat this circling activity. This went on and on for days, and it annoyed me. It appeared to be a military plane, so I called the Navy and explained the situation. The Navy said it wasn't one of their planes and referred me to the Coast Guard. I then called the Coast Guard who told me the plane was a trainer for new pilots. I explained I was a survivor of 9/11, and the plane was upsetting and frightening me. I then asked if they wouldn't mind training their pilots somewhere else. I was surprised that they obliged, and that's the last I saw or heard of that plane. This incident just proved that even in the comfort of Bodega Bay, I was on edge.

On the drive back to the desert when our house-sitting job ended, I was on red-alert in the car. Riding in the passenger seat facing west driving over the Golden Gate Bridge, my binoculars were trained westward toward Japan in case of air attack.

I wasn't thinking about what to do if a plane attacked the bridge. That was the wrong war anyway. The Japanese weren't going to come. The Golden Gate Bridge, revered by generations of San Franciscans, would remain intact.

At home in Palm Desert, I was treated with kindness and respect in almost heroic proportions. Some people even kissed and hugged me. My barber referred to me as "9/11" (and still does). Many suggested that God is not through with me yet. I often wonder what His plans are for me.

Much to my surprise, shortly after returning to Palm Desert, I was pleased to receive a check from Keith, for my "services" on 9/11 and an invitation to address his group again in New York. To express my gratitude for all he had done for me during the 9/11 time frame, I told him there would be no consulting fee for coming back for a re-engagement. However, this time the seminar and individual consultation would focus more appropriately on "improving teamwork," rather than on "inventing your future" because of what the company had recently gone through. That was fine with me.

Aftershock

I suffered from nightmares for months. My wife said they were intense. I don't remember.

The 9/11 Emergency Relief Fund and later, the Red Cross, offered free counseling and residential programs to survivors. I took advantage of both. We could even choose our recovery facility with no questions asked; cost wasn't a factor, so I picked a first rate one in Arizona, only four hours distant.

I'm sure I was a difficult patient because I didn't take instructions very well and quarreled with my counselor when she kept insisting that my wife come for family weekend. I told her my wife was not coming. Period. One morning at our daily group session the counselor reached into a drawer and pulled out a folder labeled, "Anger Management." That really pissed me off. I knew who it was for—me. The anger management counselor agreed with me that anger was not my problem. It was hers. Then they added post-traumatic shock to the things I needed to work on. So now I am a recovering alcoholic with anger management problems, interpersonal relations problems (my counselor), and post-traumatic shock syndrome. I think they added the word "syndrome" to make it sound really serious and charge more. I also remember talking to the staff psychiatrist about my sex life, and he fell asleep in his chair. I guess it wasn't as exciting to him as it was to me. I'm surprised they didn't add sex deviate to my list of maladies. It was hard to get up every day for twenty-eight days in a room of twenty drug and alcohol abusers and say, "Hello, my name is Bert. I'm an alcoholic and possibly a sex deviate suffering from post-traumatic shock with anger management issues, and today I am feeling happy, joyous and free!" However, the food was good, as were the social life and outings to the golf driving range, wall climbing and kick boxing, the latter two being new experiences for me.

Before leaving I was asked to complete a critique of my month there. The resident psychiatrist and my primary counselor did not receive good marks. At least I had learned to express my feelings as a result of my month there. In fact every morning at our group session, each of us had to look over a list of statements of how we felt that morning: were we happy, sad, glad, angry, calm, and a few others. I learned to express my feelings verbally. That alone was worth the trip. As a kid at home in Cincinnati, I wasn't encouraged to express aloud how I felt. Now I could articulate them and overcome some of the repressed feelings from 9/11. What a difference it has made in my relationships and how I feel about myself.

Sometimes people on the battlefield watch as a buddy is killed next to them and say they feel guilty because they think they should be the one to die. I didn't feel that way at all, but I wondered if the shock I suffered was at all as intense as that experienced by the American men and women in Iraq and Afghanistan, with their compatriots dying all around them. I got some insight into PTSD (post traumatic stress disorder) in an article titled, "911 and Addiction—10 Years Later," in a newsletter called "The Fix," which is excerpted below.

> *Sunday marks the 10th anniversary of 9/11. Yet the terrible toll of addiction on survivors suffering from trauma still remains only a footnote. . . .*
>
> *. . . Much of the public discussion has focused on the "meaning" of that catastrophic day in light of the decade that followed. Two endless wars and the loss of immense blood and treasure; atrocities like secret renditions and torture; absurdities like the color-coded terror alert that were, like more and more government policies generally, cynically manipulated for partisan and political ends; a financial meltdown and economic recession of a severity not seen since the Great Depression. . . .*
>
> *. . . A darkening 10 years, many Americans agree, with recent polls finding that three out of four say they and the country itself are "worse off" or "going in the wrong direction" since that fateful day. . . .*
>
> *But for some Americans — above all, those survivors who were directly exposed to the catastrophic collapse of the Twin Towers and the aftermath's long rescue-and-recovery labors at Ground Zero — 9/11 was a tragedy and a trauma of a more personal, daily and lasting order. These are people who experienced terror, captivity,*

*powerlessness; who came face to face with mortal
danger and what psychologist Robert Jay Lifton,
the pioneering theorist of Post-Traumatic Stress
Syndrome (PTSD), called "the death imprint," the
overwhelming, unassimilable presence of bloody and
burnt bodies and body parts in the hellish landscape
of ash and smoke. . . .*

*. . . Thirteen percent of the population of New
York showed signs of PTSD or depression in the wake
of 9/11. . . . Proximity to the World Trade Center
on 9/11 was found to be significantly associated
with increased alcohol consumption in the first four
months following the attacks.*

. . . Dr. Figley [Dr. Charles Figley, a professor
of disaster mental health at Tulane University]
*noted an important difference between wartime
trauma and the trauma that many suffered on 9/11:
"You go into a combat zone and then you leave. You
don't leave home. You return all the time."*

*And so it's no surprise that PTSD symptoms —
and relapses from recovery — tend to re-emerge
around important anniversaries of the traumatic
event, causing paranoia, anxiety and depression. . . .
There is no drug to treat trauma, no quick fix . . . .
However, new research shows that people who suffer
from PTSD benefit from the support of family and
friends. . . ."*

Benefitting from the support of family and friends
was true of my situation. I had (and still have) the support
of my wife, my immediate family, old friends (literally!),
and new friends. I joined the local Citizens on Patrol, an

65

extension of the Palm Desert Sheriff's Department; the Big Brothers Organization; the landscape committee of our Shadow Mountain Resort Homeowners Association, of which I was a director and vice-president; I travel worldwide on cruise ships where the social life abounds; and I surround myself with family, friends and noble activities. The hardest part of my healing process was simply getting off my butt and out of the house. My wife was helpful in this, God bless her.

Behind the Scenes

Rescue and Recovery

The rescue and recovery work following the attack on the towers was formidable and involved the resources of local and imported firefighters, police, emergency medical service personnel, hospitals and hospital ships, the U.S. military, local, state and federal agencies, rescue dogs, robots and just about anything and anyone else who came to the site to volunteer his capabilities.

Most of the leadership and coordination among the various rescue workers is attributed to Rudy Giuliani, mayor of New York, and proclaimed after 9/11 "Mayor of the United States." The Mayor obviously couldn't be everywhere at once. With no direct supervision in many of the areas, everyone was in charge of his own efforts. It was truly an amazing sight. Each person knew instinctively what was needed, pitching in relentlessly until near exhaustion.

At one point, bucket brigades were assembled to put out fires and remove debris. This involved the services of scores of New York Transit Department workers.

The gasses resulting from the smoldering debris, including the gypsum and asbestos and possible carcinogens released by the conflagration, would wreak havoc on the rescue workers' bodies for some time to come.

The World Trade Center is the only place I know of that had three name changes in two days, from "WTC" to "Ground Zero" to "the Hole," the latter having been bestowed on it by rescuers to identify what was left after the digging commenced.

Never did so many brave firefighters and police officers give their lives for the eleven who were finally rescued from the buildings.

The rescue workers' mission quickly changed from "search and rescue" to "search and identify" (bodies). In some places only piles of bones, teeth, and fragments of human tissue were left.

In addition to the human considerations, there were the physical remains of the buildings that had to be disposed of. Some 185,000 tons of structural steel were hauled away, the bulk of which was sold to China and India. The pace of the steel removal was rapid, with the majority of it removed by the end of that September. It would be another six months before metal workers and construction crews cleared the site.

Not all of the steel was recovered by rescue workers. Some of it disappeared mysteriously, as did some of the $650 million in gold and silver being kept in a special vault from floors beneath 4 World Trade Center.

Some of the steel was reserved for special purposes, one being the twenty-four tons of WTC steel that were used in the building of a warship named the *U.S.S. New York* which debuted in New York Harbor and was christened by Mayor Michael Bloomberg symbolically on July 4th, 2006.

Other scrap aluminum from the demolished towers wound up being incorporated into two Mars Rovers, named "Spirit" and "Opportunity," now located on the surface of Mars. Sometime soon the Rovers will fall silent, but their aluminum tribute to the 9/11 victims and their families will survive on the surface of Mars for millions of years to come.

Unsung Heroes

There were many unsung heroes on 9/11. Foremost among them were the New York Fire Department and the New York Police Department. Lesser known were the United States Coast Guard; the United States Navy's Military Sealift Command; other various mariners; the Air Reserve F-15 Eagles; amateur radio operators, transit workers, rescue dogs and robots.

New York Fire Department (NYFD)

Chief Joseph Pfeifer and his crew with Battalion 1 of the NYFD were among the first to arrive at the World Trade Center, setting up a command post in the lobby of the North Tower shortly before nine A.M. Due to falling debris, it was soon moved to a location across West Street. This command post was taken out when the South Tower collapsed an hour later, and moved a third time to a firehouse in Greenwich Village, making reliable transmissions nearly impossible.

The NYFD deployed two hundred units to the site. More than four hundred firefighters were on the scene as the buildings collapsed—121 engine companies, 62 ladder companies and associated units. They were joined by firefighting units from Nassau, Suffolk, Westchester Counties and elsewhere, but with limited ability to coordinate efforts.

These personnel were followed by 9/11 system ambulances and EMTs. Due to the unprecedented volume of radio traffic, EMS chiefs had difficulty getting a clear picture of what was going on and where they were needed most.

Medical supplies, including equipment for airway and vascular control were provided by local hospitals. Few patients would arrive for treatment. In the early evening, it was realized that few would survive the collapse, if any. The area was closed down.

Three hundred forty-three firefighters gave their lives trying to rescue people trapped on the stairways and elsewhere in the buildings. Many who were able to move up in the building were unable to get down to safety as the buildings collapsed from within floor by floor.

[For a riveting, captive account of the firefighters who gave generously so much for so few on 9/11, see "Report from Ground Zero" by Dennis Smith.]

New York Police Department (NYPD)

The NYPD set up its incident command post at Church and Vesey Streets on the opposite side of the WTC from where the NYFD was commanding its operations. NYPD helicopters arrived on the scene, unable to do much but report on the status of the burning buildings. Rooftop rescue was impossible. The helicopters that had reached the towers were told to return to base by the FAA or risk being shot down.

As the buildings collapsed, twenty-three NYPD officers were killed, along with thirty-seven Port Authority Police Officers.

The United States Coast Guard
and Other Mariners
"American Dunkirk"

On 9/11 after the attacks, on the other side of town, people were jamming the piers hoping to be rescued by a flotilla of ferry boats, Coast Guard vessels and civilian boats that answered a call on their radios from the Coast Guard to come to the piers on the West Side and the Battery to help in the rescue.

These rescuers were risking their lives and boats to save people they didn't know and would never see again. The expense of fuel was high, insurance coverage of an accident with an over-loaded boat was questionable, but the so-called "boatlifters" were dauntless in their determination and selflessness in saving lives. The captains and crews of many vessels, including tug boats, ferries, sightseeing and fishing boats, as well as private yachts converged on the West Side and the Battery on the southern tip of Manhattan to boatlift stranded commuters to safety. Despite the enormous number of boats and people involved, there were no major injuries reported.

The refugees were picked up from the embankments, docks and piers and removed from harm's way to Staten Island, New Jersey and Brooklyn. Some were in the water and needed to be fished out with boathooks. The trips weren't made any the less dangerous, as it was often necessary to use radar to navigate through the dust and debris from the towers which obscured visibility.

To put the West Side evacuation in perspective, in the *Miracle of Dunkirk* during WWII, it is recorded that 338,000 British and French soldiers were evacuated by sea in nine days. In New York that fateful day, it is estimated as many as 500,000 civilians were evacuated by boat in nine hours. The rescuers were too busy to take an actual count.

In 2001, on a normal working day, there were about 2.2 million commuters in New York City. Hundreds of thousands of them were blocked from leaving the city by car, rail or bus. I don't know how they heard about the "Boatlifters," as the operation was called, because I don't recall seeing it on TV. The New York exodus was not widely known at that time. People I asked about it had little or no memory of hearing about it, yet it was rescue on the grandest of scales.

In a recent ten-minute documentary called "Boatlift" by Eddie Rosenstein and hosted by Tom Hanks, Mr. Hanks is quoted as saying, "Boats, usually an afterthought in most New Yorkers' minds, were, for the first time in over a century, the only way in or out of lower Manhattan."

According to New York Waterway Captain Rick Thornton, who was involved in the escape, people were actually jumping into the river and swimming out of Manhattan, just as I had planned to do in the East River. Boats of every description and size were nearly running them over.

The massive convergence of boats was triggered by a call issued by the local Coast Guard at about 11 A.M. on

VHF 13 and 16 immediately after the collapse of the South Tower ... "All available boats, this is the United States Coast Guard aboard the pilot boat *New York*. Anyone wanting to help with the evacuation of lower Manhattan, report to Governors Island."

The Coast Guard, according to David Helvarg, President of the Blue Frontier Campaign, notes that maps showing the location of Coast Guard cutters on September 12 had formed "what looks like a belt being cinched tightly around the continental United States as the service quickly shifted from a peacetime to a wartime footing." The Coast Guard and all the civilian mariners deserve high marks for their rapid response.

This was surely "thinking out of the box" at its best. They certainly were among the unsung heroes of 9/11.

The United States Navy Sealift Command

According to *Sealift*, the U.S. Navy's Military Sealift Command Newsletter, "Just three days after the September 11, 2001, terrorist attacks on the World Trade Center, Military Sealift Command hospital ship USNS Comfort rounded the tip of Manhattan, its white profile a striking contrast against the devastating backdrop of smoke billowing from Ground Zero. For nearly three weeks, 61 civil service mariners and about 300 Navy personnel worked day and night to run a logistics support facility—complete with warm meals, hot showers, laundry services and berthing for hundreds of emergency relief personnel . . . Comfort's team of Navy psychology personnel also provided mental health consultations to relief workers from the towers."

The F-15 Eagles

In 2001, the F-15 Eagles, manufactured by McDonnell Douglas, were our first line of defense against airborne terrorists (and expected to be until 2015). Their speed and firepower are best described as "awesome." They are allowed to fly at speeds up to Mach 2 (equivalent to the speed of sound, or 1100 feet per second).

The F-15's maximum cruise speed is 761 mph at sea level and 678 mph at 30,000 feet. The perception of going at maximum speed is no different from flying at a lower speed. One is not crushed by speed, but by acceleration, adding additional risk to the pilot.

On 9/11, two fighters were airborne from Otis Air National Guard Base in Cape Cod, Massachusetts, at 8:52 a.m., barely six minutes after the North Tower was hit and eleven minutes before the second terrorist plane hit the South Tower. The lead F-15 was armed with six missiles and 940 rounds of 20 millimeter ammunition for its cannons, which could fire 100 shots per second. They were (and are) not permitted to fire on civilian aircraft without direct orders from the President and Secretary of Defense. On 9/11, the orders never came.

The fighter flying time from Otis Air Base to the WTC was approximately ten minutes. This meant they had only ten minutes to intercept Flight 175, but without the order to fire, at best they could only intercept and harass the enemy-controlled planes.

Since the terrorist planes were gone, the F-15s' main purpose that day was to clear the air of all traffic, which they did in record time, and keep the airspace free, thus insuring the safety of the skies for another day. No air accidents were reported as a result.

Transit Workers

The Mineta Transportation Institute, representing the New York City transit employees concluded that in the initial weeks after September 11, sixty percent of the rescue and recovery personnel at WCT Ground Zero were, in fact, New York City transit workers.

Amateur Radio Operators

Approximately five hundred amateur radio operators contributed to the rescue and clean-up operations. They established communications, emergency networks and bucket brigades with hundreds of other volunteers.

Alcoholics Anonymous

One of the most devastating effects of 9/11 was the staggering increase in alcoholism. By December, 2001, cities up and down the east coast were reporting an increased demand for alcohol and drug abuse treatment. A survey of 265,000 people who had been in the city on that day found that 226,000 people reported consuming more alcohol than they had in the year before the attack. By the spring of 2004 the number of NYFD firefighters and EMT workers being treated for substance abuse was fifty percent higher than in 2003.

The afternoon of September 11, in a Red Cross room near Ground Zero, two members of Alcoholics Anonymous began providing services 24/7 for recovering alcoholic rescue workers. At first, the Red Cross was reluctant to make the room available, as it was in the midst of the confusion and potential problems with the residue in the air.

As the story goes, someone in AA called President Bush and explained the problem and the need for a meeting hall. He apparently called the Red Cross and told them, "Give them the room they need." AA got the room immediately and kept it open throughout the recovery, for which the workers and their families were grateful.

On a personal note, because I am a recovered alcoholic, I had my own personal visit from AA in New Jersey. On the night of September 12, when I was staying at the Embassy Suites in Parsippany, New Jersey, I received a call from someone I had never heard of saying he had received a telephone call from Newport, Rhode Island, saying someone there had notified the local AA central office that I was nearby and might need a meeting. He mentioned he was sending some men over to pick me up and take me to a meeting. How they found me remains a mystery to this day. At 5:30 P.M., two young men arrived to pick me up to take me to the local meeting. The ride in their old, dilapidated pickup was harrowing, something I could have done without. When we arrived at Fellowship Hall, I had the same kind of feeling of security as I had when I finally reached the safety of the Club Quarters only one night earlier. I was home again with my family of recovering alcoholics.

The Rescue Dogs

On September 11, FEMA (Federal Emergency Management Agency) organized and deployed around one hundred volunteer search dogs with their handlers to help rescue workers locate stranded people in remote or threatening locations in both towers. The dogs also had the grisly task of locating human body parts.

There is no official count of the number of dogs who gave their lives to the rescue effort that day. The best I could come up with is that only twelve of them remain. The circumstances of their deaths and possibly those of their handlers are not generally known.

After September 12, no one was found alive, and the dogs were so distressed not to locate survivors that it became necessary to stage situations where "survivors" could be found by the dogs to keep up their morale.

The search-and-rescue dogs who participated in the effort came from eighteen different states. Some of their stories are told in a book by Charlotte Dumas called *Retrieved*. Ten years after 9/11, Ms. Dumas traveled across nine states from Texas to Maryland, capturing these animals in their twilight years in their homes with their handlers. [For more information, Charlotte's website is: http://www.charlottedumas.nl.]

The Robots

The story of the robots sent to "Ground Zero" at the World Trade Center site became known as an example of human kindness and ingenuity aroused by the calamity of 9/11.

Far away from New York, at Texas A&M University, Robin Murphy, a professor of computer science, and her fellow roboticists reacted quickly and contacted Joe Dyer, chief operating officer of iRobot. Professor Murphy literally pulled the robots out of the laboratory and sent them to Ground Zero.

These robots are shoe-box-sized creatures called PackBots, with tank-like tread and shipping-crane arms that can get into small spaces. It was the job of these robots to enter small spaces that defied human egress or were too hot for rescuers to search.

They would search for victims and assess the structural integrity of the debris, transmitting images back to their handlers. They had the grisly task of relaying information about body parts that could be used later by the forensics experts in identifying victims.

During those nine days, four teams of robotics experts with a total of sixteen robots, worked with firefighters and searchers, trying to find signs of life amid twisted steel beams and concrete shards.

The robot—the Micro VGTV (variable geometry tracked vehicle)—has a video camera and lights which gives its operators eyes. The robot also has an ear—a microphone—that can pick up the voice of a victim. If the victim is conscious, the robot operator can talk to the victim through a small speaker.

Tragically, no voices were heard for the next seven days. The Canadian manufacturer of the Inuktun robot, Nanaimo, said that despite the fact the robots had located five bodies, it had "mixed feelings about the discovery because the victims were not alive."

These robots are now being employed in Afghanistan and other disaster-torn areas. Two of them showed up here in Palm Desert to help in the search for pipe bombs in May, 2012.

Patriotism Abounds

Blood Donations

On September 11 and the days immediately following, blood banks across the nation were overflowing with concerned Americans who wanted to do their part for the fallen victims and rescuers. Donations soared to record levels. People lined up and waited for hours to donate blood.

According to *New York Magazine*, 36,000 units of blood were donated to the New York Blood Center alone. The country's blood banks collected close to 600,000 more units in the fall of 2001 than they would have had the attacks not taken place.

Unfortunately, since there were few survivors who required blood, over one-third of the donated blood was simply discarded because of its short shelf life.

Religious Fervor

In the days and weeks following the 9/11 attacks, religious fervor in this country hit an all-time high. The doors of churches, synagogues, temples, mosques, you name it, were packed with people looking to their gods for answers to 9/11, praying for salvation on earth and for the souls of those taken from them. All denominations, colors, creeds and races bonded together in prayer and meditation hoping this would never happen again.

September 11, 2011

Ten Years Later

It is now over ten years later. Until now, I haven't been able to handle recounting the details of the death and mayhem and reconstruct my part in the episode.

Every year around the anniversary of 9/11, my feelings of disillusionment and anger manifest themselves, especially when I read that in a closed-door House GOP meeting on June 28 of this year (2012), a congressman "likened the Supreme Court's ruling upholding the Democratic health care law to the September 11 terrorist attacks." How does he think the families of the victims and survivors feel about that? Yet, I am proud to be an American and know that our country is in safer hands than it was on 9/11/2001.

The memories of 9/11 reoccur every time I hear a big plane flying overhead. I look up if I am outside to see where it is going and how fast it is flying. I can sense or hear a distant plane even before people with normal hearing can, even with a hearing disability. I can hear them in the middle of the night. In fact, I have said to my wife who has superior hearing (what wife doesn't?), "Did you hear that?" before a plane is anywhere near. I look up and wish them well.

Each time I tell my story of the events of 9/11, I am overcome with a sense of remorse. It feels like being transported into another place at another time. Lingering on are the feelings, the loss of friends, the smell of burning buildings and human flesh, the screams, the sirens wailing their way to the rescue, the brave firemen and policemen, the sound of pounding footsteps on the pavement, and even the rescue dogs who lost their lives trying to recover human souls but instead located bodies and body parts.

People ask me if it bothers me to talk about my 9/11 experience. It does, but I say, "No, it's okay." I'm willing to talk about it only because I think that somehow it will help them. But after beginning to relate my story, they seem more interested in telling me where *they* were when they heard the news. That's okay, because it personalizes it and brings them into that awful day with me, which they seem anxious to relive vicariously. They want me to know that I am not alone. They were there in spirit, too. They want to share my grief, and I in theirs.

I want to reach out to as many people as possible, which is one reason for this book. Americans need to be warned not to let their defenses down and insist that homeland defense should be the priority issue on political agendas.

In 1958, when I was stationed at Camp Roberts, California, a former Luftwaffe pilot, who was attending the Sixth Army Rifle and Pistol Matches as a contender from a National Guard unit, told me, "Someday you'll get yours. Americans have been lucky so far. Your homeland will be invaded just like we were in Germany. Then you will have to give up your childhood innocence and grow up as a nation." He was also careful to point out that he had never shot at any American pilots on the airfields, just the planes. I didn't reply to that because I was afraid of starting another war, but in retrospect he was prescient, but he had history on his side.

In her book, *Touching History*, published in 2008, Lynn Spencer quotes a Continental Airlines pilot telling a flight attendant, "Mark the time and date, because life in America has just changed forever. This is the death of innocence." Ms. Spencer may have been prophetic, as was the Luftwaffe pilot.

Even now, ten years later, two frequently-asked questions remain: "How did the towers collapse just from the impact of two jet liners?" and "Wasn't there something else involved?" I talked to one survivor who believed that someone had placed incendiary material on several floors which produced the simultaneous flash noted on several lower floors with the impact of the planes. That would have been impossible in my opinion. How could whoever placed the explosives be able to time the ignition with the arrival of the planes—which were late taking off from Logan (and one of them even did a 180-degree turn over Cleveland)?

An exhaustive study supported by a 10,000 page scientific study by the National Institute for Standards and Technology (NIST) offers only theories about how it was possible for part of a WTC structure to fall through the path of most resistance at free-fall speed, completely violating the accepted law of physics. NIST was forced to admit that they were unable to provide a full explanation for the total collapse.

As far as I am concerned, all speculation about errors in communication at the top government levels and theories are as irrelevant now as they were then. Let's just get on with it and build a new, safer America. But . . . let's not forget.

On May 1, 2011, U.S. Special Forces (Navy Seals) attacked bin Laden's compound in Abbottabad, Pakistan, and captured and shot bin Laden point blank in the face. I saw it as anti-climactic, but it did bring some satisfaction, but no real closure. His henchmen in al-Qaeda are being culled out, which reduces the threat to our safety, including air travel, as inconvenient as it may seem. But there are more to eliminate. I won't rest peacefully until the last al-Qaeda is dead and gone to hell. There are more sacrifices we need to make.

Like many tragic or traumatic events in life that bring new perspectives to us, my participation in 9/11 has profoundly affected my psyche—in terms of my view of myself, my view of the world and my view of how I might contribute to bringing some stability and direction to humankind.

My first reaction to my involvement to 9/11 was confusion, followed by fear, followed by revenge—basically, the same as our government. Confusion was evident in the losing sight of the planes, thinking that the first hit to the North Tower was a small, private plane, and not knowing how, where and when to employ our first line of defense, the F-15s, nor who was empowered to give the order to call them up. The key elements in war of command and control seemed murky at best.

As time gets further away from 9/11, I have come to realize that my views on just about everything in life have changed—and continue to change. These changes are so profound that at times I wonder if I have lost my stability. I have become more acutely aware of the fine, almost indistinguishable line between insanity and reason. I feel for people who become unstable from a traumatic event.

It is my desire that everyone reading this will always remember the tragic day of 9/11—and like Pearl Harbor and the Holocaust—never to be forgotten. **Never. Never forgotten.** These stories need to be passed down from generation to generation with as much intensity as possible, and let the beacon on Freedom Tower at Ground Zero in New York speak for all of us who want to see the values of our forefathers restored and peace and goodwill to all people shine brightly for liberty, justice, and equality That should be our goal for the foreseeable future, supported by a government "of the people, by the people and for the people." God Bless America.

As I was sitting on our back patio of our modest villa in Palm Desert on a beautiful clear day putting the finishing touches on the final draft of my story, I noticed a pretty little brown sparrow with a white-tufted chest fly right into the large plate glass window above my head. He must have thought he was just flying along merrily in the sky. There was a "thunk" as he flew into the glass window pane which reflected the sky. He fell out of the sky and landed on his back at my feet. I watched in horror as his little legs trembled, straightened out and then stopped. He was dead. I gave him a dignified burial in our fruit orchard. This little helpless sparrow was a reminder just like 9/11 was—and still is—of how fragile and unpredictable life can be.

Mapping the Skies

Whenever I tell people about writing a book about 9/11, they invariably think I am an expert in the field I am writing about, asking questions I am not qualified to answer. I don't, therefore, claim to be an expert on the cause and effect of the terrorist attack on our homeland on September 11, 2001. For some things there are no answers, which is difficult for some people, including myself to accept. September 11 is a classic example of this.

I am pretty clear what happened to me on that longest of days of my life, but there are some aspects of it I can't ignore as they impacted on my very being. So, I researched them through the myriad of information available.

Take the subject of air intervention by F-15 fighters, for example.

Because I actually saw some of them flying over parts of New York City where the sky was not obscured by smoke, my curiosity led to even more research. I wanted to know more about how our skies were secured that day.

At 9:10 A.M. following the crash into the Twin Towers, the NORAD commander had not yet been authorized to launch the NORAD fighters to intercept the hijacked airliners. There were several conditions that delayed the launch. One was the intelligence that more than four planes were still in the sky with intentions to destroy more buildings. Even in the terrorists' planning stage, there was disagreement over how many targets to acquire; bin Laden finally persuaded his henchmen to limit the attack to four assaults. More than that would create logistical and communications problems. Apparently, the CIA wasn't aware of that at the time. They, nor anybody else, knew the exact number of terrorist takeovers. That meant there would be a great risk in having F-15 interceptors flying into heavy domestic traffic, not knowing which planes were the threats and which were not. How do the F-15 pilots know which of the hundreds of planes flying in the Northeast Corridor to bring down?

Believe me, it would be disquieting to look out the window of a plane at 30,000 feet and see a fully-armed F-15 flying alongside wondering if it has come to shoot you down.

Then there was the possibility of the high-speed fighters colliding with the slower-moving passenger planes and others.

There were many planes which had been diverted from their flight paths to reach the nearest airport. Their pre-arranged flight plans were moot.

And finally, there was the problem of mid-air refueling because of the temporary shortage of available air tankers. Once out of fuel, there is the risk of crashing into a building or neighborhood.

The FAA and NORAD had to take these obstacles into consideration in planning a defensive shield. Apparently, there was also a shortage of National Guard pilots available to pilot the F-15s. At the time, many of them were engaged in piloting commercial airliners, their full-time jobs. With the closing of airspace to domestic travel, there was no way for them to get to Otis Air National Guard Base in Massachusetts or Langley Air Force Base in Virginia from as far away as California. One Air Force general devised a plan to send a 767 around the country to pick up stranded pilots and return them to their bases.

Meanwhile, the F-15s from Otis Air Base were circling over the east coast waiting for clearance to enter New York airspace, running low on fuel flying supersonic to get to New York. There were no KC-10 tankers airborne at the time to refuel the F-15s. This meant the planes from Otis Air Base would have to be replaced by the only other aircraft on alert at Langley, three hundred plus miles to the south. Even at Mach II, it would take too much time to get there to be of value if there were more enemy jets close to their targets.

Dedicating the Otis Air Base planes to New York was of concern because it would possibly bring too much hardware into one region of the country that might be needed elsewhere. The responders didn't know yet of the attack on the Pentagon and the thwarted attack on the White House or the Capitol.

Major General Larry Arnold, NORAD Commander for the United States, decided to institute AFIO (Agreement for Fighter Interceptor Operations) to enter FAA-controlled airspace.

This would be the first time in American history that American fighters would fly a mission over America in heavy traffic and be cleared all the way to the ground.

Fortunately, none of the planes would be needed, although it was hotly debated whether or not they would have been in time to intercept the flight that passengers took down in Shanksville. Either way, the people on that plane were going to die.

All of the participants on our civil defense effort that day deserve the highest praise and thanks from a grateful America. Many of them rejected taking any rest or leave. These were people who put the country ahead of themselves. One pilot, when he finally reached his home after hours of grueling work, was greeted by his young son with the touching words, "Don't worry, Dad, we knew you would take care of it."

What Next?

When someone asks me, based on my research and study of the facts of the attack on the World Trade Center, if I think such an event will happen again. I answer, as any intelligent person would answer, that I simply do not know. I can study as much as I want to, try to separate out my personal feelings based on my involvement, and reach an impassioned rational conclusion, but then I ask myself, "Were the perpetrators of 9/11 rational people by our beliefs and standards?" Not exactly.

These terrorists don't think the same as we. To them, dying is a badge of honor in the act of killing anyone who does not share their fervent and seemingly evil values. Strangely enough, I have read that the families of the sacrificial dupes of al-Qaeda and other fanatical religious groups are compensated for the loss of their fathers, husbands and sons, and even daughters. Why would they want to compensate them for the honor of seeing their family member die for the cause?

In May of this year I conducted a survey of people who were not in the towers on 9/11. I asked if they felt any safer now than they did before 9/11, and did they think it could happen again. The answers were unanimous. One hundred percent said they feel safer, yet they all thought it could happen again.

When I look back at what happened on 9/11 and the progress we have made in wiping out al-Qaeda's leaders, our adjusting our national defense to plan for an attack generated domestically instead of from overseas, our intelligence gathering and dissemination and our destruction of the terrorist leadership, I think the chances of a major calamity are far less than they were prior to 9/11. And if it does come, it will be far different.

We captured and interrogated Khalid Sheikh Mohammed, extracting valuable information from him, much of which is classified. It was Khalid Sheikh Mohammed who is believed to have organized the September 11 attack, and not bin Laden, although it was bin Laden who gave the go-ahead to limit the attack to the four targets, instead of the ten originally planned.

Apparently the original plan was to attack ten American planes in the U.S. and simultaneously bomb aircraft in Southeast Asia. The plan changed to hijacking ten planes in the U.S. and flying them into targets here. Why ten planes, no one knows. This was not an act of kind restraint. Osama bin Laden thought this would be impractical to plan and coordinate, hence reducing the force to four planes and four targets as more manageable and more favorable to total success.

The original team of international hijackers was apparently replaced by Saudis because the Saudis had close relationships with the United States, and it would be less of a problem to get them visas to enter the United

States. Even then, on the day of the attack, three of the terrorists were delayed boarding approval by airport security until just before boarding the planes.

The actual planning for 9/11 took place over five years but required only two months of simulated practice. Since the mastermind and executioner was Khalid Sheikh Mohammed and not bin Laden, when President Bush held up the bin Laden "Wanted Dead or Alive" poster, it should have included the Sheikh. Of course, most people here knew of bin Laden, but not the Sheikh.

The reasons I advance that mitigate against a repeat of 9/11 are as follows:

- Bin Laden was captured, killed by a shot in the head and fed to the fish. His death has not been avenged by the al-Qaeda (yet), although there have been many other terrorist attacks around the world outside the U.S.

- Khalid Sheikh Mohammed was captured and interrogated, revealing all sorts of critical information into the infrastructure and planning of the al-Qaeda operation. Interestingly, five of the ten top lieutenants have been killed by drones in Afghanistan as of this writing. With the death of their leader, bin Laden, and the neutralizing of the leadership, al-Qaeda is essentially gone, according to the Associated Press report of April 27, 2012. There are splinter groups, especially Yemen's al-Qaeda in the Arabian Peninsula. Perhaps unable to conduct complex attacks in the U.S., such groups are capable of wreaking havoc overseas.

- The ten top al-Qaeda leaders have been killed since 9/11, thus decimating the ranks of those responsible for the planning, financing, and weapons acquisition.

- According to one source, six thousand al-Qaeda fighters have been killed in Iraq.
- The coalition forces and the Afghani military are gradually eliminating many of the guerilla terrorist camps in the region.
- Airport and other security is tighter in the U.S.
- None of the ten major terrorist attacks since 9/11 have occurred on U.S. territory. They have occurred in various locations in Europe and in Asia. Therefore, there is no consistent pattern in these attacks which might indicate they are not centrally planned.
- The U.S. intelligence services are talking to each other.
- A country-wide network of truck drivers has trained drivers to be on the lookout for suspicious activity on the highways and in truck stops.
- Border patrol has been heightened and circling the U.S. with Coast Guard vessels instigated, creating a shield around our borders.
- There is coordination among the various U.S. air defense agencies.
- The erection of the Freedom Tower symbolizes our will and resolve not to be intimidated by a bunch of heartless thugs.
- President Obama has made himself personally responsible for overseeing the kill list of identified terrorists. One was eliminated recently on May 4, 2012.

Timelines and Reports

9/11 Timeline

This abbreviated timeline was developed by the author from many sources which are listed under "References and Suggested Reading." It includes as nearly as I can recall what I was doing and thinking at various times during the day.

The key points for me were being there in the first place, what was happening on the streets around the towers, the sequestering in the hotel, the shutting off of water and then electricity, and the order to abandon the hotel.

These are all my personal experiences on the ground masked by smoke and what was happening in the skies. The planning for the attack went on for at least two years prior, but the real drama began at 6:00 A.M. when the terrorists were beginning to assemble.

September 11, 2001
A.M.

6:00:   The terrorists begin to assemble at Logan Airport in Boston. Mohamed Atta, ringleader of the terrorist group, travels from Portland International Jetport, Portland, Maine to Logan International Airport, accompanied by Abdulaziz al-Omari, arriving forty five minutes later.

6:52:   Marwan al-Shehhi calls Atta from another terminal at Logan to confirm that plans are set for the attack.

7:35:   Atta and al-Omari board American Airlines Flight 11.

7:40:   The other hijackers board American Airlines Flight 11.

7:59:   American Flight 11, a Boeing 767 with 10,000 gallons of jet fuel departs Boston's Logan Airport for Los Angeles, California with 81 passengers (including 5 hijackers) and 11 crew members.

8:14:   American Flight 11 has what will be its last routine radio communication with FAA's Boston Air Route Traffic Control Center.

American Flight 11 fails to heed air controller's instruction to climb to 35,000 feet. This is the first indication of trouble aboard the plane. It isn't until an hour later at 9:25 that the F-15s from Otis on Cape Cod arrive over New York City, an hour and a half after the North Tower is hit and nine minutes after the South Tower is hit.

8:14: United Flight 175, a Boing 767, departs Boston Logan Airport for Los Angeles, California, with 56 passengers (including 5 hijackers) and 9 crew members.

8:15: *Bert Upson departs from his hotel for the World Trade Center unsuspecting of any threatened attacks.*

8:19: Betty Ong, a flight attendant on American Flight 11, alerts American Airlines from the airborne plane via an air phone, ". . . I think we are being hijacked.

8:20: American Flight 77, a Boeing 757, departs Washington Dulles Airport for Los Angeles, California, with 58 passengers (including 5 hijackers) and 6 crew members.

8:21: American Flight 11 (the Boston/Logan plane) has its transponder signal turned off so there is no way traffic control can monitor its location, which means the plane has lost the ability to communicate with FAA except by radio, which is being controlled by the hijackers.

8:24: A radio transmission comes from American Flight 11, "We have some planes. Just stay quiet, and you'll be okay. We are returning to the airport." This is most likely Atta's voice, as he mistakenly holds a button directing his voice to the radio rather that to the plane's cabin. Air traffic controllers hear that transmission, as well as the next one made by Atta, "If you try to make any moves, you'll endanger yourself and the airplane." So the flight controllers knew something was amiss on that plane.

8:25:   Boston FAA Center flight controllers alert other flight control centers regarding the status of American Flight 11. NORAD is not yet alerted.

8:26:   American Flight 11 makes a 100-degree turn to the south, now heading directly for New York City.

8:34:   Dan Bueno, flight controller from Boston FAA Center notifies the tower controller at Otis Air National Guard Base at Cape Cod of the hijacking of American Flight 11. The controller at Otis directs Bueno to contact NEADS (Northeast Air Defense Sector, the northeast sector of NORAD). The controller then notifies Otis Ops Center that a call from NEADS would be coming. Two F-15 pilots are standing by and begin to suit up.

8:37:   United Flight 175 confirms that it has sighted the hijacked American Flight 11.

8:38:   Boston Center notifies NEADS of the hijacking of American Flight 11, the first notification by NORAD that American Flight 11 had been hijacked. The Boston controller requests military help to intercept the jetliner.

8:40:   NORAD is notified of the hijacking of American Flight 11 heading South over the Sands Point nuclear facility towards New York City. The question remains unanswered why the terrorists failed to select the nuclear facility as a target of opportunity that potentially would have killed millions of people and shut down New York City. Theoretically, Sands Point was impenetrable, but then, no one, including Condoleezza Rice, imagined that the Twin Towers could be hit by our own planes.

8:40: *Bert Upson arrives at the Vestek headquarters on floor 78 of the South Tower to prepare for his seminar.*

8:41: Otis Air National Guard Base personnel are directed to go to their battle stations.

8:42: United Airlines Flight 93, a Boeing 757, departs Newark, New Jersey Airport for San Francisco, California with 37 passengers (including 4 hijackers) and 7 crew members following a 40-minute delay due to congested runways. [That accounts for the last of the four hijacked planes.]

8:43: The FAA notifies NORAD that United Flight 175 from Boston to Los Angeles has also been hijacked.

8:46: NEADS scrambles two F-15 fighter jets from Otis Air National Guard Base in Falmouth, Massachusetts, with the intention of intercepting American Flight 11. Because American Flight 11's transponder is off, the pilots do not know the location of their target.

8:47: American Flight 11 with 20,000 gallons of jet fuel crashes into Tower #1, the North Tower, between floors 93 and 99, approximately 26 minutes after controllers lost contact. The aircraft enters the building mostly intact. It plows into the building core, severing all three gypsum-encased stairwells, dragging combustibles with it. A powerful shock wave occurs down to the ground and up again. *This causes the tremor Upson feels in the South Tower.* The combustibles and the remnants of the aircraft are ignited by burning fuel. People below the severed stairwells start to evacuate the building. No one above the impact zone is able to do so.

8:47:   *Upson hears a muffled explosion coming from the north side of the building. He goes to investigate but finds nothing amiss.*

8:48:   The first of at least 100 people, maybe even 250, in the North Tower begin jumping to their deaths. One firefighter is hit by a jumper and dies instantly. No form of airborne evacuation is attempted, as smoke is too dense for a successful landing on the roof, and the tarmac is too hot to walk on.

8:49:   The first network television and radio broadcasts report an explosion or incident at the World Trade Center.

8:50:   Hijacking begins on American Flight 77 on its way to Washington.

8:51:   A flight controller of the FAA's New York Center observes that United Flight 175 has changed its transponder code twice four minutes earlier. He unsuccessfully tries to contact the flight.

        NYFD establishes its Incident Command Post in the lobby of the North Tower only five minutes following the impact of American Flight 11.

8:52:   On United Flight 175 a flight attendant calls the United Airlines office in Chicago saying that the plane has been hijacked, both pilots have been killed and the hijackers are probably flying the plane.

8:52:   Two F-15s take off from Otis Air Base. They go after United Flight 175 at speeds topping 500 mph, but are unable to catch the United plane. The top speed of the F-15s is 1875 mph, or 30 miles a minute, but at those speeds they could easily overspeed Flight 175, or not be able to locate it because no one knows where it was.

8:53:   EMT personnel arrive at the North Tower.

8:54:   American Flight 77 makes an unauthorized turn to the south.

8:55:   *Upson and companion decide to evacuate the building.*

President George W. Bush arrives at Emma E. Booker Elementary School in Sarasota, Florida, when Presidential Advisor Andrew Card informs him by telephone that a small twin engine plane has crashed into the World Trade Center. Before entering the classroom, Mr. Bush gets the confirming word by telephone from Condoleezza Rice from the White House that a commercial aircraft, not a small plane has struck the WTC. . . . "That's all we know right now, Mr. President."

8:56:   The transponder on American Flight 77 is turned off, and primary radar contact with the aircraft is lost, meaning the location of the plane cannot be pinpointed with any degree of accuracy.

8:58:   *Upson and companion arrive at the exit on the 78th floor and have a choice of going down Stairway B or taking the elevator which is an express. They decide to board the elevator.*

8:58:   United Flight 175 makes a U-turn and heads towards New York City.

8:59:   *Upson and companion board elevator for what will be its last complete round trip. They reach the mezzanine exit to the building two to three minutes later, just before the second plane hits their tower.*

9:00:   Two hundred firefighters arrive at the WTC and begin climbing stairs with heavy equipment to begin rescuing people.

9:02:   Evacuation of the North Tower is ordered by the FDNY.

A manager from the FAA's New York Center tells the Air Control System Command Center in Herndon, Virginia, "We have several situations going on here. It's escalating big time. We need to get the military involved with us."

9:03:   President Bush enters the school classroom in Sarasota, Florida.

United Flight 175 smashes into #2 WTC, the South Tower, between floors 78 and 87, 43 minutes after it is reported missing, and 23 minutes after NORAD is notified. All 65 people onboard United Flight 175 die instantly on impact, as well as unknown hundreds in the building itself. The impact is so great that parts of the plane are ejected from the building on its east and north sides and fall to the ground six blocks away.

A massive evacuation of the South Tower begins below the impact zone. Stairwell B remains unblocked from the top to the bottom of the tower, but it fills rapidly with smoke.

FAA New York notifies NEADS of the hijacking of United Flight 175 which has already flown into the South Tower.

9:04:   FAA Boston Air Route Traffic Control Center stops all departures from airports in its jurisdiction of New England and eastern New York State.

9:05:   President Bush begins reading *The Pet Goat* to the students when Chief of Staff, Andrew Card, whispers to the President, "A second plane hit the second tower. America is under attack." America is now at war with terrorism according to our President.

9:11:   The last PATH train leaves the World Trade Center.

9:13:   The F-15 fighters from Otis Air Base leave military airspace off Long Island headed for Manhattan.

9:15:   New York Center advises NEADS that UA 175 was the second aircraft crashed into the WTC.

9:16:   AA headquarters is aware that American Flight 11 has crashed into the WTC.

9:17:   CBS News reports that the intelligence community suspects that Osama bin Laden is behind the attack.

9:21:   The Port Authority of Newark orders all bridges and tunnels in the metropolitan area closed.

9:24: NORAD is notified that American Flight 77 from Washington to Los Angeles has also been hijacked.

NORAD launches two F-16 fighters from Langley AFB in Virginia to intercept the airliner.

9:25: Herndon Command Center orders nationwide ground stop.

The Otis-based F-15s establish an air patrol over New York City. They are difficult to see because of the smoke caused by the burning towers, but one could hear them zooming by overhead.

9:26: The FAA orders all nonmilitary planes grounded and cancels all flights in the U.S.

9:28: Hijackers storm the cockpit on United Flight 93 and take control.

9:30: President Bush makes his first public statements about the attacks.

The New York Stock Exchange is evacuated.

Upson and companion seek refuge in the Club Quarters Hotel.

9:32: Dulles tower observes radar of fast-moving aircraft (later identified as AA 77).

9:34: FAA advises NEADS that AA 77 is missing.

9:35: The Secret Service orders the immediate evacuation of the Vice President from the White House, uneceremoniously lifting him up under the arms and transporting him downstairs to the underground security shelter.

9:35: The Secret Service orders the President's motorcade to depart from the Booker School for the Sarasota-Bradenton International Airport to board *Air Force One*. It heads the wrong way out of the school and has to stop and turn around. The Florida State Highway Patrol is concerned the President's entourage might be under attack. It takes 40 minutes for the Secret Service to get the President out of the school and onto Air Force One.

9:36: Flight attendant on UA 93 notifies UA of hijacking. UA attemps to contact cockpit.

9:37: American Flight 77 crashes into the Pentagon, 42 minutes after contact was lost and one hour after NORAD notification of the first hijacking of American Flight 11.

9:43: The White House and the Capitol are evacuated and closed.

9:45: U.S. airspace is shut down entirely with the exception of the F-15s and their refuelers. All commercial aircraft are notified to land immediately at the nearest facility. This causes some confusion and creates a problem for the F-15s and potential air accidents. Nearly all international flights headed to the U.S. are redirected to Canada, while flights from South America are redirected to Mexico. Transport Canada also closes down its airspace, launching the agency's "Operation Yellow Ribbon."

9:45: Secret Service orders complete evacuation of the White House, the Congress, Supreme Court, Justice Department, State Department, and all other federal buildings.

9:49: The FAA Command Center at Herndon, Virginia, suggests that someone at the FAA headquarters should decide whether to request military assistance with United Flight 93.

9:50: The 110-story South Tower implodes and collapses, only 47 minutes after it is hit.

9:51: FDNY Battalion Chief Orio Palmer reaches the 78th floor Sky Lobby of the South Tower along with Fire Marshall Ronald Bucca, reporting that there are two pockets of fire and numerous dead bodies.

9:57: Passenger revolt begins on United Flight 93.

9:58: An emergency dispatcher in Pennsylvania receives a call from passenger on United Flight 93 from Newark: "We are being hijacked; we are being hijacked."

10:00: Order is given by the NYFD to the firemen in the North Tower to evacuate the building.

10:02: The Sears Tower in Chicago is evacuated as a precautionary measure followed by other high density buildings and amusement parks across the nation.

10:03: United Flight 93 crashes at 563 mph, due to a struggle in the cockpit 80 miles southeast of Pittsburgh, Pennsylvania, in a place called Shanksville.

10:07: Cleveland Center advises NEADS of UA 93 hi-jacking.

10:10: The fourth and last plane is hijacked, 42 minutes after ground contact is lost and 90 minutes after NORAD notification, raising questions about the timeliness of the response of sophisticated military radar systems and jet scramble procedures.

Vice President Cheney, unaware that United Flight 93 has crashed, authorizes fighter aircraft to engage the inbound plane, reported to be 80 miles from Washington, based on speed and trajectory projections. It has disappeared from radar.

10:13: Thousands are involved in an evacuation of the United Nations Complex in New York City.

10:15: UA headquarters aware that Flight 93 has crashed in Pennsylvania. Washington Center advises NEADS that Flight 93 has crashed in Pennsylvania.

10:20: Aboard Air Force One, President Bush tells Vice President Cheney that he has authorized a shoot-down of aircraft if necessary.

10:22: The State Department, Justice Department and World Bank in Washington are evacuated.

10:24: All transatlantic aircraft flying into the U.S. are diverted to Canada.

10:28: The North Tower collapses, seventy minutes after the collision.

The Marriott Hotel, where Upson normally stays, located at the base of the North and South Towers, collapses.

10:31: NORAD communicates the Vice President's shoot-down authority to NEADS.

10:37: A 757 is reported to have crashed in western Pennsylvania.

The Mall of America in Bloomington, Minnesota, is evacuated as a precaution.

10:41: NBC News confirms a 757 is reported to have crashed in western Pennsylvania.

From a protected area of the White House, Vice President Cheney tells President Bush (on board Air Force One) not to return quickly to Washington.

10:43: CNN reports that a mass evacuation of Washington, D.C., has begun.

10:50: Five stories of the western side of the Pentagon collapse from fire damage.

11:00: Mayor Rudolf Giuliani of New York orders an evacuation of Lower Manhattan. *[This order is not received at Upson's hotel until later in the afternoon.]*

11:05: The FAA confirms that several planes have been hijacked in addition to American Flight 11.

PM

12:04: Los Angeles International Airport is evacuated.

12:15: The U.S.-Mexico and U.S.-Canada borders are closed.

12:40: *Lunch ordered into the Club Quarters Hotel from Chinatown by hotel very welcomed by all of us who had been concerned by the lack of food stored in the hotel.*

12:55: Taliban officials deny any responsibility for the attacks.

1:04: President Bush puts the U.S. Military on high alert worldwide, stating that "freedom itself was attacked this morning by a faceless coward, and freedom will be defended." U.S. embassies worldwide are ordered closed.

1:44: The Pentagon announces five warships and two aircraft carriers (the USS George Washington and the USS John F. Kennedy), along with frigates and guided missile destroyers, will leave the U.S. Naval Station in Norfolk, Virginia, to protect the East Coast from further attack.

2:30: The FAA announces no commercial aircraft will be allowed in the air until noon EST, Wednesday (September 12) at the earliest.

2:39: At a press conference in New York, Mayor Rudy Giuliani is asked to estimate the number of casualties at the World Trade Center. He replies, "More than any of us can bear."

2:49: New York Mayor Giuliani restores partial subway and bus service in New York City.

2:50: President Bush flies to Offutt AFB in Nebraska.

3:30: *Hotel Club Quarters' water is shut down.*

4:10: The 47-story #7 World Trade Center building complex is reported to be on fire.

4:30: *Hotel Club Quarters' electricity is turned off.*

4:35: *Upson evacuates his sanctuary and heads east to find the Lexington Avenue subway on the other side of town.*

5:20: The #7 World Trade Center collapses. It has already been evacuated.

6:54: President Bush arrives at the White House, despite the fact the Secret Service had ordered its evacuation at 9:45 that morning.

7:00: Efforts to locate survivors in the rubble that had been the towers continue. Fleets of ambulances are lined up to transport the injured to nearby hospitals, but stand empty.

8:30: President Bush addresses the nation from the White House. Among his statements he says, "The search is underway for those who are behind these evil acts... we will make no distinction between the terrorists who committed these acts and those who harbor them."

11:30: President enters into his journal before going to sleep, "The Pearl Harbor of the 21st century took place today — we think it's Osama bin Laden."

As reported in the 9/11 Commission Report, following are timelines for the four individual airline flights: American Airlines Flight 11 (AA 11), United Airlines Flight 175 (UA 175), American Airlines Flight 77 (AA 77), and United Airlines Flight 93 (UA 93).

In honor of the surviving families, American Airlines and United Airlines have retired the flight numbers of these four planes.

American Airlines Flight 11 (AA 11)
Boston to Los Angeles

7:59	Takeoff
8:14	Last routine radio communication; likely takeover
8:19	Flight attendant notifies AA of hijacking
8:21	Transponder is turned off
8:23	AA attempts to contact the cockpit
8:25	Boston Center aware of hijacking
8:38	Boston Center notifies NEADS of hijacking
8:46	NEADS scrambles Otis Air Base fighter jets in search of AA 11
8:46:40	AA 11 crashes into 1 WTC (North Tower)
8:53	Otis fighter jets airborne
9:16	AA headquarters aware that Flight 11 has crashed into WTC
9:21	Boston Center advises NEADS that AA 11 is airborne heading for Washington
9:24	NEADS scrambles Langley fighter jets in search of AA 11

United Airlines Flight 175 (UA 175)
Boston to Los Angeles

8:14	Takeoff
8:42	Last radio communication
8:42-46	Likely takeover
8:47	Transponder code changes
8:52	Flight attendant notifies UA of hijacking
8:54	UA attempts to contact the cockpit
8:55	New York Center suspects hijacking
9:03:11	Flight 175 crashes into 2 WTC (South Tower)
9:15	New York Center advises NEADS that UA 175 was the second aircraft crashed into WTC
9:20	UA headquarters aware that UA 175 had crashed into WTC

American Airlines Flight 77 (AA 77)
Washington, D.C. to Los Angeles

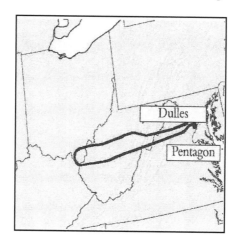

8:20	Takeoff
8:51	Last routine radio communication
8:51-54	Likely takeover
8:54	Flight 77 makes unauthorized turn to south
8:56	Transponder is turned off
9:05	AA headquarters aware that AA 77 is hijacked
9:25	Herndon Command Center orders nationwide ground stop
9:32	Dulles tower observes radar of fast-moving aircraft (later identified as AA 77)
9:34	FAA advises NEADS that AA 77 is missing
9:37:46	AA 77 crashes into the Pentagon
10:30	AA headquarters confirms AA 77 crash into Pentagon

United Airlines Flight 93 (UA 93)
Newark to San Francisco

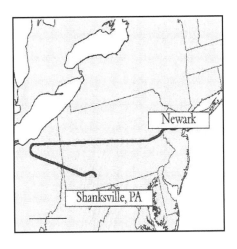

8:42	Takeoff
9:24	Flight 93 receives warning from UA about possible cockpit intrusion
9:27	Last routine radio communication
9:28	Likely takeover
9:34	Herndon Command Center advises FAA headquarters that UA 93 is hijacked
9:36	Flight attendant notifies UA of hijacking; UA attempts to contact the cockpit
9:41	Transponder is turned off
9:57	Passenger revolt begins
10:03:11	Flight 93 crashes in field in Shanksville, PA
10:07	Cleveland Center advises NEADS of UA 93 hijacking
10:15	UA headquarters aware that Flight 93 has crashed in PA; Washington Center advises NEADS that UA 93 has crashed in PA

The 9/11 Rescue Boats

The author wishes to thank Captain John Doswell of the Working Harbor Committee for permission to print the following list of 9/11 rescue boats, which was compiled by him a year after 9/11 and updated through August 2011. If the reader knows of a boat that participated in the rescue effort but is missing from the list, please contact John at. John@WorkingHarbor.org.

ABC-1, Reynolds Shipyard, Tug Boat
Abraham Lincoln, NY Waterway, Ferry Boat
Adriatic Sea, K-Sea Transportation Corp., Tug Boat
Alexander Hamilton, NY Waterway, Ferry Boat
Amberjack V, Amberjack V, Fishing Boat
American Legion, New York City Department of
    Transportation, Ferry Boat
Barbara Miller, Miller's Launch, Tug Boat
Barker Boys, Barker Marine Ltd., Tug Boat
Bayleen, Pegasus Restoration Project, Historic Whaleboat
Bergen Point, Ken's Marine, Tug Boat
Bernadette, Hudson River Park Trust, Work Boat

Blue Thunder, United States Merchant Marine Academy, Sportfisherman
Bravest, NY Fast Ferry, Ferry Boat
Brendan Turecamo, Moran Towing Corp., Tug Boat
Bruce A. McAllister, McAllister Towing & Transportation, Tug Boat
Capt. John, John Connell, Unknown
Captain Dann, Dann Ocean Towing, Tug Boat
Catherine Turecamo, Moran Towing Corp., Tug Boat
Chelsea Screamer, Kennedy Engine Company, Inc., Sightseeing Vessel
Chesapeake, Unknown, Unknown
Christopher Columbus, NY Waterway, Ferry Boat
Circle Line VIII, Circle Line/World Yacht, Sightseeing Vessel
Circle Line XI, Circle Line/World Yacht, Sightseeing Vessel
Circle Line XII, Circle Line/World Yacht, Sightseeing Vessel
Circle Line XV, Circle Line/World Yacht, Sightseeing Vessel
Circle Line XVI, Circle Line/World Yacht, Sightseeing Vessel
Coral Sea, K-Sea Transportation Corp., Tug Boat
Diana Moran, Moran Towing Corp., Tug Boat
Dottie J, United States Merchant Marine Academy, Sportfisherman
Driftmaster, US Army Corps of Engineers, Skimmer
Eileen McAllister, McAllister Towing & Transportation, Tug Boat
Elizabeth Weeks, Weeks Marine Inc., Tug Boat
Emily Miller, Miller's Launch, Tug Boat

Empire State, NY Waterway, Ferry Boat
Excaliber, VIP Yacht Cruises, Dinner/Cruise Vessel
Express Explorer, Express Marine, Tug Boat
Finest, NY Fast Ferry, Ferry Boat
Fiorello La Guardia, NY Waterway, Ferry Boat
Fire Fighter, FDNY, Fireboat
Frank Sinatra, NY Waterway, Ferry Boat
Franklin Reinauer, Reinauer Transportation Company,
   Tug Boat
Garden State, NY Waterway, Ferry Boat
Gelberman, US Army Corps of Engineers, Work Vessel
George Washington, NY Waterway, Ferry Boat
Giovanni Da Verrazano, NY Waterway, Ferry Boat
Gov. Herbert H. Lehman, New York City Department of
   Transportation, Ferry Boat
Growler, United States Merchant Marine Academy,
   USCG Tug
Gulf Guardian, Skaugen Petro Trans Inc., Tug Boat
Hatton, US Army Corps of Engineers, Work Vessel
Hayward, US Army Corps of Engineers, Work Vessel
Henry Hudson, NY Waterway, Ferry Boat
Horizon, VIP Yacht Cruises, Dinner/Cruise Vessel
Hurricane I, United States Merchant Marine Academy,
   Utility
Hurricane II, United States Merchant Marine Academy,
   Utility
JC, Unknown, Unknown
Jersey City Police Emergency Service Unit Boat, Jersey
   City Police Emergency Service, Police Boat
John D. McKean, FDNY, Fireboat
John F. Kennedy, New York City Department of
   Transportation, Ferry Boat

John J. Harvey, John J. Harvey, Ltd, retired FDNY
    Fireboat
John Jay, NY Waterway, Ferry Boat
John Reinauer, Reinauer Transportation Company, Tug
    Boat
Kathleen Turecamo, Moran Towing Corp., Tug Boat
Kathleen Weeks, Weeks Marine Inc, Tug Boat
Ken Johnson, Interport Pilot Agency, Pilot Boat
Kevin C. Kane, FDNY, Fireboat
Kimberley Turecamo, Moran Towing Corp., Tug Boat
Kings Pointer, US Merchant Marine Academy, Training
    Vessel
Kristy Ann Reinauer, Reinauer Transportation Company,
    Tug Boat
Lady, Ron Santee, Unknown
Launch No. 5, USCG Auxiliary, Former Police Launch
Lexington, Lexington Classic Cruises, Dinner/Cruise
    Vessel
Little Lady, Little Lady Water Taxi, Ferry Boat
Margaret Moran, Moran Towing Corp., Tug Boat
Marie J. Turecamo, Moran Towing Corp., Tug Boat
Mariner III, Kennedy Engine Company, Inc, Dinner/
    Cruise Vessel
Mary Alice, DonJon Marine Co. Inc, Tug Boat
Mary Gellately, Gellately Petroleum and Towing, Tug Boat
Mary L. McAllister, McAllister Towing & Transportation,
    Tug Boat
Maryland, K-Sea Transportation Corp, Tug Boat
Maverick, United States Merchant Marine Academy,
    Pilot Launch
McAllister Sisters, McAllister Towing & Transportation,
    Tug Boat

Millennium, Fox Navigation, Ferry Boat
Miller Girls, Miller's Launch, Tug Boat
Miriam Moran, Moran Towing Corp., Tug Boat
Miss Circle Line, Circle Line - Statue of Liberty Ferry,
    Inc., Sightseeing Vessel
Miss Ellis Island, Circle Line - Statue of Liberty Ferry,
    Inc., Sightseeing Vessel
Morgan Reinauer, Reinauer Transportation Company,
    Tug Boat
Nancy Moran, Moran Towing Corp., Tug Boat
New Jersey, NY Waterway, Ferry Boat
Ocean Explorer, Unknown, Unknown
Odin, K-Sea Transportation Corp., Tug Boat
Paul Andrew, DonJon Marine Co. Inc., Tug Boat
Penn II, Penn Maritime, Tug Boat
Peter Gellately, Gellately Petroleum and Towing, Tug Boat
Pilot Boat New York, Sandy Hook Pilots Assn., Pilot Boat
Port Service, Leevac Marine (now Hornbeck Offshore
    Transportation), Tug Boat
Poseidon, United States Merchant Marine Academy,
    Patrol Boat
Potomac, Unknown, Unknown
Powhatten, DonJon Marine Co. Inc., Tug Boat
Queen of Hearts, Promoceans / Affairs Afloat, Dinner/
    Cruise Vessel
Resolute, McAllister Towing & Transportation, Tug Boat
Robert Fulton, NY Waterway, Ferry Boat
Robert Livingston, NY Waterway, Ferry Boat
Romantica, VIP Yacht Cruises, Dinner/Cruise Vessel
Royal Princess, VIP Yacht Cruises, Dinner/Cruise Vessel
Safety III, United States Merchant Marine Academy,
    Utility

Safety IV, United States Merchant Marine Academy,
   Utility Samantha Miller, Miller's Launch, Tug Boat
Sandy G, UTV Warren George, Inc., Unknown
Sassacus, Fox Navigation, Ferry Boat
Sea Service, Leevac Marine (now Hornbeck Offshore
   Transportation), Tug Boat
Seastreak Brooklyn, SeaStreak America, Inc., Ferry Boat
Seastreak Liberty, SeaStreak America, Inc., Ferry Boat
SeaStreak Manhattan, SeaStreak America, Inc., Ferry Boat
Seastreak New York, SeaStreak America, Inc., Ferry Boat
Smoke II, FDNY, Fireboat
Spartan Service, Leevac Marine (now Hornbeck Offshore
   Transportation), Tug Boat
Spirit of New Jersey, Spirit Cruises, Dinner/Cruise
   Vessel
Spirit of New York, Spirit Cruises, Dinner/Cruise Vessel
Spirit of the Hudson, Spirit Cruises, Dinner/Cruise
   Vessel
Stapleton Service, Leevac Marine (now Hornbeck
   Offshore Transportation), Tug Boat
Star of Palm Beach, Promoceans / Affairs Afloat, Dinner/
   Cruise Vessel
Sterling, Lady Liberty Cruises, Dinner/Cruise Vessel
Storm, United States Merchant Marine Academy, Search
   & Rescue
Susan Miller, Miller's Launch, Tug Boat
Tatobam, Fox Navigation, Ferry Boat
Taurus, K-Sea Transportation Corp., Tug Boat
Tender for Tugboat Bertha, Darren Vigilant, Motor Boat
Theodore Roosevelt, NY Waterway, Ferry Boat
Turecamo Boys, Moran Towing Corp., Tug Boat
Turecamo Girls, Moran Towing Corp., Tug Boat

Twin Tube, Reynolds Shipyard, Tug Boat
Unknown, USCG, 47' Motor Lifeboat
USCG tug Hawser, USCG, 65' small harbor tug (WYTL)
USCG tug Line, USCG, 65' small harbor tug (WYTL)
USCG tug Wire, USCG, 65' small harbor tug (WYTL)
USCGC Adak, USCG, 110' Island Cutter Class patrol
   boats (WPB)
USCGC Bainbridge Island, USCG, 110' Island Cutter
   Class patrol boats (WPB)
USCGC Katherine Walker, USCG, Cutter
USCGC Penobscot Bay, USCG, 140' Bay Class icebreaking
   tugs (WTGB)
USCGC Ridley, USCG, Cutter
USCGC Sturgeon Bay, USCG, 140' Bay Class icebreaking
   tugs (WTGB)
USCGC Tahoma, USCG, Cutter
Various DEC boats, DEC, Work Boats
Various fishing boats, unknown, unknown
Various Nassau County boats, Nassau County, police/
   patrol boats
Various New Jersey state and local boats, New Jersey,
   police/patrol boats
Various NYPD, NYPD, police/patrol boats
Various other vessels, unknown, unknown
Various, USCG, 41' utility boats (UTB)
Various, USCG, rigid hull inflatables (RHI)
Virginia Weeks, Weeks Marine Inc., Tug Boat
Vivian Roehrig, C & R Harbor Towing, Tug Boat
West New York, NY Waterway, Ferry Boat
Wings of the Morning, United States Merchant Marine
   Academy, Utility
Yogi Berra, NY Waterway, Ferry Boat

THE 9/11 COMMISSION REPORT

Final Report of the
National Commission on Terrorist
Attacks upon the United States

EXECUTIVE SUMMARY

COMMISSION
MEMBERS

Thomas H. Kean

CHAIR

Lee H. Hamilton

VICE CHAIR

Richard Ben-Veniste

Bob Kerrey

Fred F. Fielding

John F. Lehman

Jamie S. Gorelick

Timothy J. Roemer

Slade Gorton

James R. Thompson

COMMISSION STAFF

Philip Zelikow, Executive Director
Christopher A. Kojm, Deputy Executive Director
Daniel Marcus, General Counsel

Joanne M.Accolla
Staff Assistant
Alexis Albion
Professional Staff Member
Scott H.Allan,Jr.
Counsel
John A.Azzarello
Counsel
Caroline Barnes
Professional Staff Member
Warren Bass
Professional Staff Member
Ann M. Bennett
Information Control Officer
Mark S. Bittinger
Professional Staff Member
Madeleine Blot
Counsel
Antwion M. Blount
Systems Engineer
Sam Brinkley
Professional Staff Member
Geoffrey Scott Brown
Research Assistant

Daniel Byman
Professional Staff Member
Dianna Campagna
Manager of Operations
Samuel M.W.Caspersen
Counsel
Melissa A. Coffey
Staff Assistant
Lance Cole
Consultant
Marquittia L. Coleman
Staff Assistant
Marco A. Cordero
Professional Staff Member
Rajesh De
Counsel
George W.Delgrosso
Investigator
Gerald L. Dillingham
Professional Staff Member
Thomas E. Dowling
Professional Staff Member
Steven M. Dunne
Deputy General Counsel

Thomas R. Eldridge
Counsel
Alice Falk
Editor
John J. Farmer, Jr.
Senior Counsel & Team Leader
Alvin S. Felzenberg
Deputy for Communications
Lorry M. Fenner
Professional Staff Member
Susan Ginsburg
Senior Counsel & Team Leader
T. Graham Giusti
Security Officer
Nicole Marie Grandrimo
Professional Staff Member
Douglas N. Greenburg
Counsel
Barbara A. Grewe
Sr. Counsel, Special Projects
Elinore Flynn Hartz
Family Liaison
Leonard R. Hawley
Professional Staff Member
L. Christine Healey
Senior Counsel & Team Leader
Karen Heitkotter
Executive Secretary
Walter T. Hempel II
Professional Staff Member
C. Michael Hurley
Sr. Counsel & Team Leader

Dana J. Hyde
Counsel
John W.Ivicic
Security Officer
Michael N. Jacobson
Counsel
Hunter W.Jamerson
Intern
Bonnie D. Jenkins
Counsel
Reginald F. Johnson
Staff Assistant
R.William Johnstone
Professional Staff Member
Stephanie L. Kaplan
Special Assistant &
Managing Editor
Miles L. Kara, Sr.
Professional Staff Member
Janice L. Kephart
Counsel
Hyon Kim
Counsel
Katarzyna Kozaczuk
Financial Assistant
Gordon Nathaniel
Lederman
Counsel
Daniel J. Leopold
Staff Assistant
Sarah Webb Linden
Professional Staff Member

Douglas J. MacEachin
Professional Staff Member &
Team Leader
Ernest R. May
Senior Adviser
Joseph McBride
Intern
James Miller
Professional Staff Member
Kelly Moore
Professional Staff Member
Charles M. Pereira
Professional Staff Member
John Raidt
Professional Staff Member
John Roth
Senior Counsel & Team Leader
Peter Rundlet
Counsel
Lloyd D. Salvetti
Professional Staff Member
Kevin J. Scheid
Professional Staff Member &
Team Leader
Kevin Shaeffer
Professional Staff Member

Tracy J. Shycoff
Deputy for Administration
& Finance
Dietrich L. Snell
Senior Counsel & Team
Leader
Jonathan DeWees Stull
Communications Assistant
Lisa Marie Sullivan
Staff Assistant
Quinn John Tamm, Jr.
Professional Staff Member
Catharine S. Taylor
Staff Assistant
Yoel Tobin
Counsel
Emily Landis Walker
Professional Staff Member
& Family Liaison
Garth Wermter
Senior IT Consultant
Serena B.Wille
Counsel
Peter Yerkes
Public Affairs Assistant

THE 9/11 COMMISSION REPORT

EXECUTIVE SUMMARY

EXECUTIVE SUMMARY

WE PRESENT THE NARRATIVE of this report and the recommendations that flow from it to the President of the United States, the United States Congress, and the American people for their consideration. Ten Commissioners— five Republicans and five Democrats chosen by elected leaders from our nation's capital at a time of great partisan division—have come together to present this report without dissent.

We have come together with a unity of purpose because our nation demands it. September 11, 2001, was a day of unprecedented shock and suffering in the history of the United States. The nation was unprepared.

A NATION TRANSFORMED

At 8:46 on the morning of September 11, 2001, the United States became a nation transformed.

An airliner traveling at hundreds of miles per hour and carrying some 10,000 gallons of jet fuel plowed into the North Tower of the World Trade Center in Lower Manhattan. At 9:03, a second airliner hit the South Tower. Fire and smoke billowed upward. Steel, glass, ash, and bodies fell below. The Twin Towers, where up to 50,000 people worked each day, both collapsed less than 90 minutes later.

At 9:37 that same morning, a third airliner slammed into the western face of the Pentagon. At 10:03, a fourth airliner crashed in a field in southern Pennsylvania. It had been aimed at the United States Capitol or the White House, and was forced down by heroic passengers armed with the knowledge that America was under attack.

More than 2,600 people died at the World Trade Center; 125 died at the Pentagon; 256 died on the four planes. The death toll surpassed that at Pearl Harbor in December 1941.

This immeasurable pain was inflicted by 19 young Arabs acting at the behest of Islamist extremists headquartered in distant Afghanistan. Some had been in the United States for more than a year, mixing with the rest of the population. Though four had training as pilots, most were not well-educated. Most spoke English poorly, some hardly at all. In groups of four or five, carrying with them only small knives, box cutters, and cans of Mace or pepper spray, they had hijacked the four planes and turned them into deadly guided missiles.

Why did they do this? How was the attack planned and conceived? How did the U.S. government fail to anticipate and prevent it? What can we do in the future to prevent similar acts of terrorism?

A Shock, Not a Surprise

The 9/11 attacks were a shock, but they should not have come as a surprise. Islamist extremists had given plenty of warning that they meant to kill Americans indiscriminately and in large numbers. Although Usama Bin Ladin [sic] himself would not emerge as a signal threat until the late 1990s, the threat of Islamist terrorism grew over the decade.

In February 1993, a group led by Ramzi Yousef tried to bring down the World Trade Center with a truck bomb. They killed six and wounded a thousand. Plans by Omar Abdel Rahman and others to blow up the Holland and Lincoln tunnels and other New York City landmarks were frustrated when the plotters were arrested. In October 1993, Somali tribesmen shot down U.S. helicopters, killing 18 and wounding 73 in an incident that came to be known as "Black Hawk down." Years later it would be learned that those Somali tribesmen had received help from al Qaeda.

In early 1995, police in Manila uncovered a plot by Ramzi Yousef to blow up a dozen U.S. airliners while they were flying over the Pacific. In November 1995, a car bomb exploded outside the office of the U.S. program manager for the Saudi National Guard in Riyadh, killing five Americans and two others. In June 1996, a truck bomb demolished the Khobar Towers apartment complex in Dhahran, Saudi Arabia, killing 19 U.S. servicemen and wounding hundreds. The attack was carried out primarily by Saudi Hezbollah, an organization that had received help from the government of Iran.

Until 1997, the U.S. intelligence community viewed Bin Ladin as a financier of terrorism, not as a terrorist leader. In February 1998, Usama Bin Ladin and four others issued a self-styled fatwa, publicly declaring that it was God's decree that every Muslim should try his utmost to kill any American, military or civilian, anywhere in the world, because of American "occupation" of Islam's holy places and aggression against Muslims.

In August 1998, Bin Ladin's group, al Qaeda, carried out near-simultaneous truck bomb attacks on the U.S. embassies in Nairobi, Kenya, and Dar es Salaam, Tanzania. The attacks killed 224 people, including 12 Americans, and wounded thousands more.

In December 1999, Jordanian police foiled a plot to bomb hotels and other sites frequented by American tourists, and a U.S. Customs agent arrested Ahmed

Ressam at the U.S. Canadian border as he was smuggling in explosives intended for an attack on Los Angeles International Airport.

In October 2000, an al Qaeda team in Aden, Yemen, used a motorboat filled with explosives to blow a hole in the side of a destroyer, the USS Cole, almost sinking the vessel and killing 17 American sailors.

The 9/11 attacks on the World Trade Center and the Pentagon were far more elaborate, precise, and destructive than any of these earlier assaults. But by September 2001, the executive branch of the U.S. government, the Congress, the news media, and the American public had received clear warning that Islamist terrorists meant to kill Americans in high numbers.

Who Is the Enemy?
Who is this enemy that created an organization capable of inflicting such horrific damage on the United States? We now know that these attacks were carried out by various groups of Islamist extremists. The 9/11 attack was driven by Usama Bin Ladin.

In the 1980s, young Muslims from around the world went to Afghanistan to join as volunteers in a jihad (or holy struggle) against the Soviet Union. A wealthy Saudi, Usama Bin Ladin, was one of them. Following the defeat of the Soviets in the late 1980s, Bin Ladin and others formed al Qaeda to mobilize jihads elsewhere.

The history, culture, and body of beliefs from which Bin Ladin shapes and spreads his message are largely unknown to many Americans. Seizing on symbols of Islam's past greatness, he promises to restore pride to people who consider themselves the victims of successive foreign masters. He uses cultural and religious allusions to the holy Qur'an and some of its interpreters. He appeals to people disoriented by cyclonic change as they confront modernity and globalization. His rhetoric selectively draws from multiple sources—Islam, history, and the region's political and economic malaise.

Bin Ladin also stresses grievances against the United States widely shared in the Muslim world. He inveighed against the presence of U.S. troops in Saudi Arabia, which is the home of Islam's holiest sites, and against other U.S. policies in the Middle East.

Upon this political and ideological foundation, Bin Ladin built over the course of a decade a dynamic and lethal organization. He built an infrastructure and organization in Afghanistan that could attract, train, and use recruits against ever more ambitious targets. He rallied new zealots and new money with each demonstration of al Qaeda's capability. He had forged a close alliance with the Taliban, a regime providing sanctuary for al Qaeda.

By September 11, 2001, al Qaeda possessed

- leaders able to evaluate, approve, and supervise the planning and direction of a major operation;
- a personnel system that could recruit candidates, indoctrinate them, vet them, and give them the necessary training;
- communications sufficient to enable planning and direction of operatives and those who would be helping them;
- an intelligence effort to gather required information and form assessments of enemy strengths and weaknesses;

- the ability to move people great distances; and
- the ability to raise and move the money necessary to finance an attack.

1998 to September 11, 2001

The August 1998 bombings of U.S. embassies in Kenya and Tanzania established al Qaeda as a potent adversary of the United States.

After launching cruise missile strikes against al Qaeda targets in Afghanistan and Sudan in retaliation for the embassy bombings, the Clinton administration applied diplomatic pressure to try to persuade the Taliban regime in Afghanistan to expel Bin Ladin. The administration also devised covert operations to use CIA-paid foreign agents to capture or kill Bin Ladin and his chief lieutenants. These actions did not stop Bin Ladin or dislodge al Qaeda from its sanctuary.

By late 1998 or early 1999, Bin Ladin and his advisers had agreed on an idea brought to them by Khalid Sheikh Mohammed (KSM) called the "planes operation." It would eventually culminate in the 9/11 attacks. Bin Ladin and his chief of operations, Mohammed Atef, occupied undisputed leadership positions atop al Qaeda. Within al Qaeda, they relied heavily on the ideas and enterprise of strong-willed field commanders, such as KSM, to carry out worldwide terrorist operations.

KSM claims that his original plot was even grander than those carried out on 9/11—ten planes would attack targets on both the East and West coasts of the United States. This plan was modified by Bin Ladin, KSM said, owing to its scale and complexity. Bin Ladin provided KSM with four initial operatives for suicide plane attacks within the United States, and in the fall of 1999 training for the attacks began. New recruits included four from a cell of expatriate Muslim extremists who had clustered together in Hamburg, Germany. One became the tactical commander of the operation in the United States: Mohamed Atta.

U.S. intelligence frequently picked up reports of attacks planned by al Qaeda. Working with foreign security services, the CIA broke up some al Qaeda cells. The core of Bin Ladin's organization nevertheless remained intact. In December 1999, news about the arrests of the terrorist cell in Jordan and the arrest of a terrorist at the U.S.-Canadian border became part of a "millennium alert." The government was galvanized, and the public was on alert for any possible attack.

In January 2000, the intense intelligence effort glimpsed and then lost sight of two operatives destined for the "planes operation." Spotted in Kuala Lumpur, the pair were lost passing through Bangkok. On January 15, 2000, they arrived in Los Angeles.

Because these two al Qaeda operatives had spent little time in the West and spoke little, if any, English, it is plausible that they or KSM would have tried to identify, in advance, a friendly contact in the United States. We explored suspicions about whether these two operatives had a support network of accomplices in the United States. The evidence is thin—simply not there for some cases, more worrisome in others.

We do know that soon after arriving in California, the two al Qaeda operatives sought out and found a group of ideologically like-minded Muslims with roots in Yemen and Saudi Arabia, individuals mainly associated with a young Yemeni and others who attended a mosque in San

Diego. After a brief stay in Los Angeles about which we know little, the al Qaeda operatives lived openly in San Diego under their true names. They managed to avoid attracting much attention.

By the summer of 2000, three of the four Hamburg cell members had arrived on the East Coast of the United States and had begun pilot training. In early 2001, a fourth future hijacker pilot, Hani Hanjour, journeyed to Arizona with another operative, Nawaf al Hazmi, and conducted his refresher pilot training there. A number of al Qaeda operatives had spent time in Arizona during the 1980s and early 1990s.

During 2000, President Bill Clinton and his advisers renewed diplomatic efforts to get Bin Ladin expelled from Afghanistan. They also renewed secret efforts with some of the Taliban's opponents — the Northern Alliance — to get enough intelligence to attack Bin Ladin directly. Diplomatic efforts centered on the new military government in Pakistan, and they did not succeed. The efforts with the Northern Alliance revived an inconclusive and secret debate about whether the United States should take sides in Afghanistan's civil war and support the Taliban's enemies. The CIA also produced a plan to improve intelligence collection on al Qaeda, including the use of a small, unmanned airplane with a video camera, known as the Predator.

After the October 2000 attack on the USS Cole, evidence accumulated that it had been launched by al Qaeda operatives, but without confirmation that Bin Ladin had given the order. The Taliban had earlier been warned that it would be held responsible for another Bin Ladin attack on the United States. The CIA described its findings as a "preliminary judgment"; President Clinton and his chief advisers told us they were waiting for a conclusion before deciding whether to take military action. The military alternatives remained unappealing to them.

The transition to the new Bush administration in late 2000 and early 2001 took place with the Cole issue still pending. President George W. Bush and his chief advisers accepted that al Qaeda was responsible for the attack on the Cole, but did not like the options available for a response.

Bin Ladin's inference may well have been that attacks, at least at the level of the Cole, were risk free.

The Bush administration began developing a new strategy with the stated goal of eliminating the al Qaeda threat within three to five years.

During the spring and summer of 2001, U.S. intelligence agencies received a stream of warnings that al Qaeda planned, as one report put it, "something very, very, very big." Director of Central Intelligence George Tenet told us, "The system was blinking red."

Although Bin Ladin was determined to strike in the United States, as President Clinton had been told and President Bush was reminded in a Presidential Daily Brief article briefed to him in August 2001, the specific threat information pointed overseas. Numerous precautions were taken overseas. Domestic agencies were not effectively mobilized. The threat did not receive national media attention comparable to the millennium alert.

While the United States continued disruption efforts around the world, its emerging strategy to eliminate the al Qaeda threat was to include an enlarged covert action program in Afghanistan, as well as diplomatic strategies for Afghanistan and Pakistan. The process culminated during the summer of 2001 in a draft presidential directive and arguments about the Predator aircraft, which was soon to be deployed with a missile of its own, so that it might be used to attempt to kill Bin Ladin or his chief lieutenants. At a September 4 meeting, President Bush's chief advisers approved the draft directive of the strategy and endorsed the concept of arming the Predator. This directive on the al Qaeda strategy was awaiting President Bush's signature on September 11, 2001.

Though the "planes operation" was progressing, the plotters had problems of their own in 2001. Several possible participants dropped out; others could not gain entry into the United States (including one denial at a port of entry and visa denials not related to terrorism). One of the eventual pilots may have considered abandoning the planes operation. Zacarias Moussaoui, who showed up at a flight training school in Minnesota, may have been a candidate to replace him.

Some of the vulnerabilities of the plotters become clear in retrospect. Moussaoui aroused suspicion for seeking fast-track training on how to pilot large jet airliners. He was arrested on August 16, 2001, for violations of immigration regulations. In late August, officials in the intelligence community realized that the terrorists spotted in Southeast Asia in January 2000 had arrived in the United States.

These cases did not prompt urgent action. No one working on these late leads in the summer of 2001 connected them to the high level of threat reporting. In the words of one official, no analytic work foresaw the lightning that could connect the thundercloud to the ground.

As final preparations were under way during the summer of 2001, dissent emerged among al Qaeda leaders in Afghanistan over whether to proceed. The Taliban's chief, Mullah Omar, opposed attacking the United States. Although facing opposition from many of his senior lieutenants, Bin Ladin effectively overruled their objections, and the attacks went forward.

September 11, 2001
The day began with the 19 hijackers getting through a security checkpoint system that they had evidently analyzed and knew how to defeat. Their success rate in penetrating the system was 19 for 19. They took over the four flights, taking advantage of air crews and cockpits that were not prepared for the contingency of a suicide hijacking.

On 9/11, the defense of U.S. air space depended on close interaction between two federal agencies: the Federal Aviation Administration (FAA) and North American Aerospace Defense Command (NORAD). Existing protocols on 9/11 were unsuited in every respect for an attack in which hijacked planes were used as weapons.

What ensued was a hurried attempt to improvise a defense by civilians who had never handled a hijacked aircraft that attempted to disappear, and by a military unprepared for the transformation of commercial aircraft into weapons of mass destruction.

A shootdown authorization was not communicated to the NORAD air defense sector until 28 minutes after United 93 had crashed in Pennsylvania. Planes were scrambled, but ineffectively, as they did not know where to go or what targets they were to intercept. And once the shootdown order was given, it was not communicated to the pilots. In short, while leaders in Washington believed that the fighters circling above them had been instructed to "take out" hostile aircraft, the only orders actually conveyed to the pilots were to "ID type and tail."

Like the national defense, the emergency response on 9/11 was necessarily improvised.

In New York City, the Fire Department of New York, the New York Police Department, the Port Authority of New York and New Jersey, the building employees, and the occupants of the buildings did their best to cope with the effects of almost unimaginable events — unfolding furiously over 102 minutes. Casualties were nearly 100 percent at and above the impact zones and were very high among first responders who stayed in danger as they tried to save lives. Despite weaknesses in preparations for disaster, failure to achieve unified incident command, and inadequate communications among responding agencies, all but approximately one hundred of the thousands of civilians who worked below the impact zone escaped, often with help from the emergency responders.

At the Pentagon, while there were also problems of command and control, the emergency response was generally effective. The Incident Command System, a formalized management structure for emergency response in place in the National Capital Region, overcame the inherent complications of a response across local, state, and federal jurisdictions.

Operational Opportunities

We write with the benefit and handicap of hindsight. We are mindful of the danger of being unjust to men and women who made choices in conditions of uncertainty and in circumstances over which they often had little control.

Nonetheless, there were specific points of vulnerability in the plot and opportunities to disrupt it. Operational failures—opportunities that were not or could not be exploited by the organizations and systems of that time—included

- not watchlisting future hijackers Hazmi and Mihdhar, not trailing them after they traveled to Bangkok, and not informing the FBI about one future hijacker's U.S. visa or his companion's travel to the United States;
- not sharing information linking individuals in the Cole attack to Mihdhar;
- not taking adequate steps in time to find Mihdhar or Hazmi in the United States;
- not linking the arrest of Zacarias Moussaoui, described as interested in flight training for the purpose of using an airplane in a terrorist act, to the heightened indications of attack;
- not discovering false statements on visa applications;
- not recognizing passports manipulated in a fraudulent manner;
- not expanding no-fly lists to include names from terrorist watchlists;
- not searching airline passengers identified by the computer-based CAPPS screening system; and
- not hardening aircraft cockpit doors or taking other measures to prepare for the possibility of suicide hijackings.

GENERAL FINDINGS

Since the plotters were flexible and resourceful, we cannot know whether any single step or series of steps would have defeated them. What we can say with confidence is that none of the measures adopted by the U.S. government from 1998 to 2001 disturbed or even delayed the progress of the al Qaeda plot. Across the government, there were failures of imagination, policy, capabilities, and management.

Imagination

The most important failure was one of imagination. We do not believe leaders understood the gravity of the threat. The terrorist danger from Bin Ladin and al Qaeda was not a major topic for policy debate among the public, the media, or in the Congress. Indeed, it barely came up during the 2000 presidential campaign.

Al Qaeda's new brand of terrorism presented challenges to U.S. governmental institutions that they were not well-designed to meet. Though top officials all told us that they understood the danger, we believe there was uncertainty among them as to whether this was just a new and especially venomous version of the ordinary terrorist threat the United States had lived with for decades, or it was indeed radically new, posing a threat beyond any yet experienced.

As late as September 4, 2001, Richard Clarke, the White House staffer long responsible for counterterrorism policy coordination, asserted that the government had not yet made up its mind how to answer the question:"Is al Qaeda a big deal?"

A week later came the answer.

Policy

Terrorism was not the overriding national security concern for the U.S. government under either the Clinton or the pre-9/11 Bush administration.

The policy challenges were linked to this failure of imagination. Officials in both the Clinton and Bush administrations regarded a full U.S. invasion of Afghanistan as practically inconceivable before 9/11.

Capabilities

Before 9/11, the United States tried to solve the al Qaeda problem with the capabilities it had used in the last stages of the Cold War and its immediate aftermath. These capabilities were insufficient. Little was done to expand or reform them.

The CIA had minimal capacity to conduct paramilitary operations with its own personnel, and it did not seek a large-scale expansion of these capabilities before 9/11. The CIA also needed to improve its capability to collect intelligence from human agents.

At no point before 9/11 was the Department of Defense fully engaged in the mission of countering al Qaeda, even though this was perhaps the most dangerous foreign enemy threatening the United States.

America's homeland defenders faced outward. NORAD itself was barely able to retain any alert bases at all. Its planning scenarios occasionally considered the danger of hijacked aircraft being guided to American targets, but only aircraft that were coming from overseas.

The most serious weaknesses in agency capabilities were in the domestic arena. The FBI did not have the capability to link the collective knowledge of agents in the field to national priorities. Other domestic agencies deferred to the FBI.

FAA capabilities were weak. Any serious examination of the possibility of a suicide hijacking could have suggested changes to fix glaring vulnerabilities—expanding no-fly lists, searching passengers identified by the CAPPS screening system, deploying federal air marshals domestically, hardening cockpit doors, alerting air crews to a different kind of hijacking possibility than they had been trained to expect. Yet the FAA did not adjust either its own training or training with NORAD to take account of threats other than those experienced in the past.

Management

The missed opportunities to thwart the 9/11 plot were also symptoms of a broader inability to adapt the way government manages problems to the new challenges of the twenty-first century. Action officers should have been able to draw on all available knowledge about al Qaeda in the government.

Management should have ensured that information was shared and duties were clearly assigned across agencies, and across the foreign-domestic divide.

There were also broader management issues with respect to how top leaders set priorities and allocated resources. For instance, on December 4, 1998, DCI Tenet issued a directive to several CIA officials and the DDCI for Community Management, stating: "We are at war. I want no resources or people spared in this effort, either inside CIA or the Community." The memorandum had little overall effect on mobilizing the CIA or the intelligence community. This episode indicates the limitations of the DCI's authority over the direction of the intelligence community, including agencies within the Department of Defense.

The U.S. government did not find a way of pooling intelligence and using it to guide the planning and assignment of responsibilities for joint operations involving entities as disparate as the CIA, the FBI, the State Department, the military, and the agencies involved in homeland security.

SPECIFIC FINDINGS

Unsuccessful Diplomacy

Beginning in February 1997, and through September 11, 2001, the U.S. government tried to use diplomatic pressure to persuade the Taliban regime in Afghanistan to stop being a sanctuary for al Qaeda, and to expel Bin Ladin to a country where he could face justice. These efforts included warnings and sanctions, but they all failed.

The U.S. government also pressed two successive Pakistani governments to demand that the Taliban cease providing a sanctuary for Bin Ladin and his organization and, failing that, to cut off their support for the Taliban. Before 9/11, the United States could not find a mix of incentives and pressure that would persuade Pakistan to reconsider its fundamental relationship with the Taliban.

From 1999 through early 2001, the United States pressed the United Arab Emirates, one of the Taliban's only travel and financial outlets to the outside world, to break off ties and enforce sanctions, especially those related to air travel to Afghanistan. These efforts achieved little before 9/11.

Saudi Arabia has been a problematic ally in combating Islamic extremism. Before 9/11, the Saudi and U.S. governments did not fully share intelligence information or develop an adequate joint effort to track and disrupt the finances of the al Qaeda organization. On the other hand, government officials of Saudi Arabia at the highest levels worked closely with top U.S. officials in major initiatives to solve the Bin Ladin problem with diplomacy.

Lack of Military Options
In response to the request of policymakers, the military prepared an array of limited strike options for attacking Bin Ladin and his organization from May 1998 onward. When they briefed policymakers, the military presented both the pros and cons of those strike options and the associated risks. Policymakers expressed frustration with the range of options presented.

Following the August 20, 1998, missile strikes on al Qaeda targets in Afghanistan and Sudan, both senior military officials and policymakers placed great emphasis on actionable intelligence as the key factor in recommending or deciding to launch military action against Bin Ladin and his organization. They did not want to risk significant collateral damage, and they did not want to miss Bin Ladin and thus make the United States look weak while making Bin Ladin look strong. On three specific occasions in 1998–1999, intelligence was deemed credible enough to warrant planning for possible strikes to kill Bin Ladin. But in each case the strikes did not go forward, because senior policymakers did not regard the intelligence as sufficiently actionable to offset their assessment of the risks.

The Director of Central Intelligence, policymakers, and military officials expressed frustration with the lack of actionable intelligence. Some officials inside the Pentagon, including those in the special forces and the counterterrorism policy office, also expressed frustration with the lack of military action. The Bush administration began to develop new policies toward al Qaeda in 2001, but military plans did not change until after 9/11.

Problems within the Intelligence Community

The intelligence community struggled throughout the 1990s and up to 9/11 to collect intelligence on and analyze the phenomenon of transnational terrorism. The combination of an overwhelming number of priorities, flat budgets, an outmoded structure, and bureaucratic rivalries resulted in an insufficient response to this new challenge.

Many dedicated officers worked day and night for years to piece together the growing body of evidence on al Qaeda and to understand the threats. Yet, while there were many reports on Bin Laden and his growing al Qaeda organization, there was no comprehensive review of what the intelligence community knew and what it did not know, and what that meant. There was no National Intelligence Estimate on terrorism between 1995 and 9/11.

Before 9/11, no agency did more to attack al Qaeda than the CIA. But there were limits to what the CIA was able to achieve by disrupting terrorist activities abroad and by using proxies to try to capture Bin Ladin and his lieutenants in Afghanistan. CIA officers were aware of those limitations. To put it simply, covert action was not a silver bullet. It was important to engage proxies in Afghanistan and to build various capabilities so that if an opportunity presented itself, the CIA could act on it. But for more than three years, through both the late Clinton and early Bush administrations, the CIA relied on proxy forces, and there was growing frustration within the CIA's Counterterrorist Center and in the National Security Council staff with the lack of results. The development of the Predator and the push to aid the Northern Alliance were products of this frustration.

Problems in the FBI
From the time of the first World Trade Center attack in 1993, FBI and Department of Justice leadership in Washington and New York became increasingly concerned about the terrorist threat from Islamist extremists to U.S. interests, both at home and abroad. Throughout the 1990s, the FBI's counterterrorism efforts against international terrorist organizations included both intelligence and criminal investigations. The FBI's approach to investigations was case-specific, decentralized, and geared toward prosecution. Significant FBI resources were devoted to after-the-fact investigations of major terrorist attacks, resulting in several prosecutions.

The FBI attempted several reform efforts aimed at strengthening its ability to prevent such attacks, but these reform efforts failed to implement organization-wide institutional change. On September 11, 2001, the FBI was limited in several areas critical to an effective preventive counterterrorism strategy. Those working counterterrorism matters did so despite limited intelligence collection and strategic analysis capabilities, a limited capacity to share information both internally and externally, insufficient training, perceived legal barriers to sharing information, and inadequate resources.

Permeable Borders and Immigration Controls

There were opportunities for intelligence and law enforcement to exploit al Qaeda's travel vulnerabilities. Considered collectively, the 9/11 hijackers

- included known al Qaeda operatives who could have been watchlisted;
- presented passports manipulated in a fraudulent manner;
- presented passports with suspicious indicators of extremism;
- made detectable false statements on visa applications;
- made false statements to border officials to gain entry into the United States; and
- violated immigration laws while in the United States.

Neither the State Department's consular officers nor the Immigration and Naturalization Service's inspectors and agents were ever considered full partners in a national counterterrorism effort. Protecting borders was not a national security issue before 9/11.

Permeable Aviation Security

Hijackers studied publicly available materials on the aviation security system and used items that had less metal content than a handgun and were most likely permissible. Though two of the hijackers were on the U.S. TIPOFF terrorist watchlist, the FAA did not use TIPOFF data. The hijackers had to beat only one layer of security — the security checkpoint process. Even though several hijackers were selected for extra screening by the CAPPS system, this led only to greater scrutiny of their checked baggage. Once on board, the hijackers were faced with aircraft personnel who were trained to be nonconfrontational in the event of a hijacking.

Financing

The 9/11 attacks cost somewhere between $400,000 and $500,000 to execute. The operatives spent more than $270,000 in the United States. Additional expenses included travel to obtain passports and visas, travel to the United States, expenses incurred by the plot leader and facilitators outside the United States, and expenses incurred by the people selected to be hijackers who ultimately did not participate.

The conspiracy made extensive use of banks in the United States. The hijackers opened accounts in their own names, using passports and other identification documents. Their transactions were unremarkable and essentially invisible amid the billions of dollars flowing around the world every day.

To date, we have not been able to determine the origin of the money used for the 9/11 attacks. Al Qaeda had many sources of funding and a pre-9/11 annual budget estimated at $30 million. If a particular source of funds had dried up, al Qaeda could easily have found enough money elsewhere to fund the attack.

An Improvised Homeland Defense

The civilian and military defenders of the nation's airspace—FAA and NORAD—were unprepared for the attacks launched against them. Given that lack of preparedness, they attempted and failed to improvise an effective home-land defense against an unprecedented challenge.

The events of that morning do not reflect discredit on operational personnel. NORAD's Northeast Air Defense Sector personnel reached out for information and made the best judgments they could based on the information they received. Individual FAA controllers, facility managers, and command center managers were creative and agile in recommending a nationwide alert, ground-stopping local traffic, ordering all aircraft nationwide to land, and executing that unprecedented order flawlessly.

At more senior levels, communication was poor. Senior military and FAA leaders had no effective communication with each other. The chain of command did not function well. The President could not reach some senior officials. The Secretary of Defense did not enter the chain of command until the morning's key events were over. Air National Guard units with different rules of engagement were scrambled without the knowledge of the President, NORAD, or the National Military Command Center.

Emergency Response

The civilians, firefighters, police officers, emergency medical technicians, and emergency management professionals exhibited steady determination and resolve under horrifying, overwhelming conditions on 9/11. Their actions saved lives and inspired a nation.

Effective decisionmaking in New York was hampered by problems in command and control and in internal communications. Within the Fire Department of New

York, this was true for several reasons: the magnitude of the incident was unforeseen; commanders had difficulty communicating with their units; more units were actually dispatched than were ordered by the chiefs; some units self-dispatched; and once units arrived at the World Trade Center, they were neither comprehensively accounted for nor coordinated. The Port Authority's response was hampered by the lack both of standard operating procedures and of radios capable of enabling multiple commands to respond to an incident in unified fashion. The New York Police Department, because of its history of mobilizing thousands of officers for major events requiring crowd control, had a technical radio capability and protocols more easily adapted to an incident of the magnitude of 9/11.

Congress

The Congress, like the executive branch, responded slowly to the rise of transnational terrorism as a threat to national security. The legislative branch adjusted little and did not restructure itself to address changing threats. Its attention to terrorism was episodic and splintered across several committees. The Congress gave little guidance to executive branch agencies on terrorism, did not reform them in any significant way to meet the threat, and did not systematically perform robust oversight to identify, address, and attempt to resolve the many problems in national security and domestic agencies that became apparent in the aftermath of 9/11.

So long as oversight is undermined by current congressional rules and resolutions, we believe the American people will not get the security they want and need. The United States needs a strong, stable, and capable congressional committee structure to give America's national intelligence agencies oversight, support, and leadership.

Are We Safer?

Since 9/11, the United States and its allies have killed or captured a majority of al Qaeda's leadership; toppled the Taliban, which gave al Qaeda sanctuary in Afghanistan; and severely damaged the organization. Yet terrorist attacks continue. Even as we have thwarted attacks, nearly everyone expects they will come. How can this be?

The problem is that al Qaeda represents an ideological movement, not a finite group of people. It initiates and inspires, even if it no longer directs. In this way it has transformed itself into a decentralized force. Bin Ladin may be limited in his ability to organize major attacks from his hideouts. Yet killing or capturing him, while extremely important, would not end terror. His message of inspiration to a new generation of terrorists would continue.

Because of offensive actions against al Qaeda since 9/11, and defensive actions to improve homeland security, we believe we are safer today. But we are not safe. We therefore make the following recommendations that we believe can make America safer and more secure.

RECOMMENDATIONS

Three years after 9/11, the national debate continues about how to protect our nation in this new era. We divide our recommendations into two basic parts: What to do, and how to do it.

WHAT TO DO? A GLOBAL STRATEGY

The enemy is not just "terrorism." It is the threat posed specifically by Islamist terrorism, by Bin Ladin and others who draw on a long tradition of extreme intolerance within a minority strain of Islam that does not distinguish politics from religion, and distorts both.

The enemy is not Islam, the great world faith, but a perversion of Islam. The enemy goes beyond al Qaeda to include the radical ideological movement, inspired in part by al Qaeda, that has spawned other terrorist groups and violence. Thus our strategy must match our means to two ends: dismantling the al Qaeda network and, in the long term, prevailing over the ideology that contributes to Islamist terrorism.

The first phase of our post-9/11 efforts rightly included military action to topple the Taliban and pursue al Qaeda. This work continues. But long-term success demands the use of all elements of national power: diplomacy, intelligence, covert action, law enforcement, economic policy, foreign aid, public diplomacy, and homeland defense. If we favor one tool while neglecting others, we leave ourselves vulnerable and weaken our national effort.

What should Americans expect from their government? The goal seems unlimited: Defeat terrorism anywhere in the world. But Americans have also been told to expect the worst: An attack is probably coming; it may be more devastating still.

Vague goals match an amorphous picture of the enemy. Al Qaeda and other groups are popularly described as being all over the world, adaptable, resilient, needing little higher-level organization, and capable of anything. It is an image of an omnipotent hydra of destruction. That image lowers expectations of government effectiveness.

It lowers them too far. Our report shows a determined and capable group of plotters. Yet the group was fragile and occasionally left vulnerable by the marginal, unstable people often attracted to such causes. The enemy made mistakes. The U.S. government was not able to capitalize on them.

No president can promise that a catastrophic attack like that of 9/11 will not happen again. But the American people are entitled to expect that officials will have realistic objectives, clear guidance, and effective organization. They are entitled to see standards for performance so they can judge, with the help of their elected representatives, whether the objectives are being met.

We propose a strategy with three dimensions: (1) attack terrorists and their organizations, (2) prevent the continued growth of Islamist terrorism, and (3) protect against and prepare for terrorist attacks.

Attack Terrorists and Their Organizations

- Root out sanctuaries. The U.S. government should identify and prioritize actual or potential terrorist sanctuaries and have realistic country or regional strategies for each, utilizing every element of national power and reaching out to countries that can help us.

- Strengthen long-term U.S. and international commitments to the future of Pakistan and Afghanistan.

- Confront problems with Saudi Arabia in the open and build a relationship beyond oil, a relationship that both sides can defend to their citizens and includes a shared commitment to reform.

Prevent the Continued Growth of Islamist Terrorism
In October 2003, Secretary of Defense Donald Rumsfeld asked if enough was being done "to fashion a broad integrated plan to stop the next generation of terrorists." As part of such a plan, the U.S. government should

- Define the message and stand as an example of moral leadership in the world. To Muslim parents, terrorists like Bin Ladin have nothing to offer their children but visions of violence and death. America and its friends have the advantage—our vision can offer a better future.

- Where Muslim governments, even those who are friends, do not offer opportunity, respect the rule of law, or tolerate differences, then the United States needs to stand for a better future.

- Communicate and defend American ideals in the Islamic world, through much stronger public diplomacy to reach more people, including students and leaders outside of government. Our efforts here should be as strong as they were in combating closed societies during the Cold War.

- Offer an agenda of opportunity that includes support for public education and economic openness.

- Develop a comprehensive coalition strategy against Islamist terrorism, using a flexible contact group of leading coalition governments and fashioning a common coalition approach on issues like the treatment of captured terrorists.

- Devote a maximum effort to the parallel task of countering the proliferation of weapons of mass destruction.

- Expect less from trying to dry up terrorist money and more from following the money for intelligence, as a tool to hunt terrorists, understand their networks, and disrupt their operations.

Protect Against and Prepare for Terrorist Attacks

- Target terrorist travel, an intelligence and security strategy that the 9/11 story showed could be at least as powerful as the effort devoted to terrorist finance.

- Address problems of screening people with biometric identifiers across agencies and governments, including our border and transportation systems, by designing a comprehensive screening system that addresses common problems and sets common standards. As standards spread, this necessary and ambitious effort could dramatically strengthen the world's ability to intercept individuals who could pose catastrophic threats.

- Quickly complete a biometric entry-exit screening system, one that also speeds qualified travelers.

- Set standards for the issuance of birth certificates and sources of identification, such as driver's licenses.

- Develop strategies for neglected parts of our transportation security system. Since 9/11, about 90 percent of the nation's $5 billion annual investment in transportation security has gone to aviation, to fight the last war.

- In aviation, prevent arguments about a new computerized profiling system from delaying vital improvements in the "no-fly" and "automatic selectee" lists. Also, give priority to the improvement of check-point screening.

- Determine, with leadership from the President, guidelines for gathering and sharing information in the new security systems that are needed, guidelines that integrate safeguards for privacy and other essential liberties.

- Underscore that as government power necessarily expands in certain ways, the burden of retaining such powers remains on the executive to demonstrate the value of such powers and ensure adequate supervision of how they are used, including a new board to oversee the implementation of the guidelines needed for gathering and sharing information in these new security systems.

- Base federal funding for emergency preparedness solely on risks and vulnerabilities, putting New York City and Washington, D.C., at the top of the current list. Such assistance should not remain a program for general revenue sharing or pork-barrel spending.

- Make homeland security funding contingent on the adoption of an incident command system to strengthen teamwork in a crisis, including a regional approach. Allocate more radio spectrum and improve connectivity for public safety communications, and encourage wide-spread adoption of newly developed standards for private-sector emergency preparedness — since the private sector controls 85 percent of the nation's critical infrastructure.

HOW TO DO IT? A DIFFERENT WAY OF ORGANIZING GOVERNMENT

The strategy we have recommended is elaborate, even as presented here very briefly. To implement it will require a government better organized than the one that exists today, with its national security institutions designed half a century ago to win the Cold War. Americans should not settle for incremental, ad hoc adjustments to a system created a generation ago for a world that no longer exists.

Our detailed recommendations are designed to fit together. Their purpose is clear: to build unity of effort across the U.S. government. As one official now serving on the front lines overseas put it to us:"One fight, one team."

We call for unity of effort in five areas, beginning with unity of effort on the challenge of counterterrorism itself:

- unifying strategic intelligence and operational planning against Islamist terrorists across the foreign-domestic divide with a National Counterterrorism Center;

- unifying the intelligence community with a new National Intelligence Director;

- unifying the many participants in the counterterrorism effort and their knowledge in a network-based information sharing system that transcends traditional governmental boundaries;

- unifying and strengthening congressional oversight to improve quality and accountability; and

- strengthening the FBI and homeland defenders. Unity of Effort: A National Counterterrorism Center The 9/11 story teaches the value of integrating strategic intelligence from all sources into joint operational planning—with both dimensions spanning the foreign-domestic divide.

- In some ways, since 9/11, joint work has gotten better. The effort of fighting terrorism has flooded over many of the usual agency boundaries because of its sheer quantity and energy. Attitudes have changed. But the problems of coordination have multiplied. The Defense Department alone has three unified commands (SOCOM, CENTCOM, and NORTHCOM) that deal with terrorism as one of their principal concerns.

• Much of the public commentary about the 9/11 attacks has focused on "lost opportunities." Though characterized as problems of "watch-listing," "information sharing," or "connecting the dots," each of these labels is too narrow. They describe the symptoms, not the disease.

• Breaking the older mold of organization stovepiped purely in executive agencies, we propose a National Counterterrorism Center (NCTC) that would borrow the joint, unified command concept adopted in the 1980s by the American military in a civilian agency, combining the joint intelligence function alongside the operations work.

• The NCTC would build on the existing Terrorist Threat Integration Center and would replace it and other terrorism "fusion centers" within the government. The NCTC would become the authoritative knowledge bank, bringing information to bear on common plans. It should task collection requirements both inside and outside the United States.

• The NCTC should perform joint operational planning, assigning lead responsibilities to existing agencies and letting them direct the actual execution of the plans.

- Placed in the Executive Office of the President, headed by a Senate-confirmed official (with rank equal to the deputy head of a cabinet department) who reports to the National Intelligence Director, the NCTC would track implementation of plans. It would be able to influence the leadership and the budgets of the counterterrorism operating arms of the CIA, the FBI, and the departments of Defense and Homeland Security.

- The NCTC should not be a policymaking body. Its operations and planning should follow the policy direction of the president and the National Security Council.

Unity of Effort: A National Intelligence Director
Since long before 9/11—and continuing to this day—the intelligence community is not organized well for joint intelligence work. It does not employ common standards and practices in reporting intelligence or in training experts overseas and at home. The expensive national capabilities for collecting intelligence have divided management. The structures are too complex and too secret.

- The community's head—the Director of Central Intelligence—has at least three jobs: running the CIA, coordinating a 15-agency confederation, and being the intelligence analyst-in-chief to the president. No one person can do all these things.

- A new National Intelligence Director should be established with two main jobs: (1) to oversee national intelligence centers that combine experts from all the collection disciplines against common targets — like counterterrorism or nuclear proliferation; and (2) to oversee the agencies that contribute to the national intelligence program, a task that includes setting common standards for personnel and information technology.

- The national intelligence centers would be the unified commands of the intelligence world — a long-overdue reform for intelligence comparable to the 1986 Goldwater-Nichols law that reformed the organization of national defense. The home services — such as the CIA, DIA, NSA, and FBI — would organize, train, and equip the best intelligence professionals in the world, and would handle the execution of intelligence operations in the field.

[See original report for organizational chart]

- This National Intelligence Director (NID) should be located in the Executive Office of the President and report directly to the president, yet be confirmed by the Senate. In addition to overseeing the National Counterterrorism Center described above (which will include both the national intelligence center for terrorism and the joint operations planning effort), the NID should have three deputies:

  - For foreign intelligence (a deputy who also would be the head of the CIA)

  - For defense intelligence (also the under secretary of defense for intelligence)

- For homeland intelligence (also the executive assistant director for intelligence at the FBI or the under secretary of homeland security for information analysis and infrastructure protection)

- The NID should receive a public appropriation for national intelligence, should have authority to hire and fire his or her intelligence deputies, and should be able to set common personnel and information technology policies across the intelligence community.

- The CIA should concentrate on strengthening the collection capabilities of its clandestine service and the talents of its analysts, building pride in its core expertise.

- Secrecy stifles oversight, accountability, and information sharing. Unfortunately, all the current organizational incentives encourage over-classification. This balance should change; and as a start, open information should be provided about the overall size of agency intelligence budgets.

Unity of Effort: Sharing Information
The U.S. government has access to a vast amount of information. But it has a weak system for processing and using what it has. The system of "need to know" should be replaced by a system of "need to share."

- The President should lead a government-wide effort to bring the major national security institutions into the information revolution, turning a mainframe system into a decentralized network. The obstacles are not technological. Official after official has urged us to call attention to problems with the unglamorous "back office" side of government operations.

• But no agency can solve the problems on its own — to build the net-work requires an effort that transcends old divides, solving common legal and policy issues in ways that can help officials know what they can and cannot do. Again, in tackling information issues, America needs unity of effort.

Unity of Effort: Congress
Congress took too little action to adjust itself or to restructure the executive branch to address the emerging terrorist threat. Congressional oversight for intelligence — and counterterrorism — is dysfunctional. Both Congress and the executive need to do more to minimize national security risks during transitions between administrations.

• For intelligence oversight, we propose two options: either a joint committee on the old model of the Joint Committee on Atomic Energy or a single committee in each house combining authorizing and appropriating committees. Our central message is the same: the intelligence committees cannot carry out their oversight function unless they are made stronger, and thereby have both clear responsibility and accountability for that oversight.

- Congress should create a single, principal point of oversight and review for homeland security. There should be one permanent standing committee for homeland security in each chamber.

- We propose reforms to speed up the nomination, financial reporting, security clearance, and confirmation process for national security officials at the start of an administration, and suggest steps to make sure that incoming administrations have the information they need.

Unity of Effort: Organizing America's Defenses in the United States
We have considered several proposals relating to the future of the domestic intelligence and counterterrorism mission. Adding a new domestic intelligence agency will not solve America's problems in collecting and analyzing intelligence within the United States. We do not recommend creating one.

- We propose the establishment of a specialized and integrated national security workforce at the FBI, consisting of agents, analysts, linguists, and surveillance specialists who are recruited, trained, rewarded, and retained to ensure the development of an institutional culture imbued with a deep expertise in intelligence and national security.

At several points we asked: Who has the responsibility for defending us at home? Responsibility for America's national defense is shared by the Department of Defense, with its new Northern Command, and by the Department of Homeland Security. They must have a clear delineation of roles, missions, and authority.

- The Department of Defense and its oversight committees should regularly assess the adequacy of Northern Command's strategies and planning to defend against military threats to the homeland.

- The Department of Homeland Security and its oversight committees should regularly assess the types of threats the country faces, in order to determine the adequacy of the government's plans and the readiness of the government to respond to those threats.

We call on the American people to remember how we all felt on 9/11, to remember not only the unspeakable horror but how we came together as a nation — one nation. Unity of purpose and unity of effort are the way we will defeat this enemy and make America safer for our children and grandchildren.

We look forward to a national debate on the merits of what we have recommended, and we will participate vigorously in that debate.

A NEW TYPE OF WAR

The Story of the FAA and NORAD Response
to the September 11, 2001 Attacks

[Prefatory Note to the 2011 Rutgers Law Review Publication:

[As the team on the 9/11 Commission Staff responsible for reconstructing the facts of the day itself, Team 8 was scrupulous to heed the direction of Commission Chairman Kean and Vice-Chairman Hamilton that we present the facts as we found them as objectively as possible. In the closing days of our work, it became clear that the most objective way to present those facts—and to capture both the urgency with which decisions were being made that day and the level of command at which critical decision making was occurring—would be to allow, where possible, the various officials and others responsible for responding to the attacks to speak for themselves. Accordingly, the team prepared what we called an "audio monograph" of critical communications from the morning of 9/11, linked by narrative and graphics placing each audio clip in context. We believed that such a rendering would be the best way to enable the public to understand what happened on 9/11—how the day was lived by those responding to the attacks.

[The raw material that went into our reconstruction of the day was not obtained easily. The Commission had heard testimony early on that no tapes were made, and we were told at one point that a technical malfunction would prevent us from hearing them. If we had not pushed as hard as we did—ultimately persuading the Commission to use its subpoena power to obtain the records—many of the critical conversations from that morning may have been lost to history.

[Before we had a chance to finalize the audio monograph, however, we were informed that there was insufficient time to put the document through the declassification process before the Commission's term expired. This was not surprising. The declassification process had been frustrating for virtually the entire Commission staff. We were forced to abandon the audio monograph and turn to writing a monograph that did not include the audio clips, and to drafting our portions of the Final Report.

[Thanks to the tireless effort of Staff Member Miles Kara, the draft monograph has now been released by the National Archives, as have the audio clips embedded in it. Miles—who our team awarded the Gold Headphones award at the completion of our work for his determination to hear everything on record from that morning—completed transcriptions of each clip, and worked with a team from Rutgers Law Review to validate those transcripts. Both the original draft and the annotated 2011 document could not have been produced without him. The Law

Review staff, assisted by Andrea Manna of the Law School administration, then worked to embed the audio clips into the text, so that the monograph can be experienced interactively.

[Because the original audio monograph was left in draft form, I have thought it appropriate to annotate it in certain instances in the interest of accuracy or completeness. Every annotation is set forth clearly in brackets. I have attempted, however, to leave the audio monograph as much as possible in its original form, as an artifact of the work of Team 8. Although the audio monograph was never formally released, virtually all of its conclusions were adopted by the 9/11 Commission. The passage of time has not diminished the value of our work, or the honor I feel at having worked and become friends with such an extraordinary group of people.]

John J. Farmer Jr.
Dean, Rutgers School of Law — Newark
Former Senior Counsel, National Commission
on Terrorist Attacks Upon the United States

CONTENTS

Staff List

Preface

7. ANOTHER MISTAKEN REPORT: DELTA
FLIGHT 1989

8. UNITED 93
8.1 FAA Awareness
8.2 Military Notification and Respond
8.3 Commission Findings and Assessment

9. THE IMPACT OF INACCURATE STATEMENTS

10. CONCLUSION

COMMISSION STAFF
RESPONSIBLE FOR THIS REPORT

John J. Farmer, Jr., *Senior Counsel & Team Leader*

John A. Azzarello, *Counsel*

Miles L. Kara, Sr., *Professional Staff Member*

Kevin Shaeffer, *Professional Staff Member*

Geoffrey Scott Brown, *Research Assistant*

Dana J. Hyde, *Counsel*

Lisa Marie Sullivan, *Staff Assistant*

Charles M. Pereira, *Professional Staff Member*

DRAFT
PREFACE

Team 8 of the National Commission on Terrorist Attacks Upon the United States has determined the operational facts of the Federal Aviation Administration's (FAA) and North American Aerospace Defense Command's (NORAD) response to [the] September 11, 2001 terrorist attacks, as reconstructed from primary sources such as logs, tape recordings, transcripts and radar data, and corroborated in interviews with key personnel involved. Set forth in this monograph is the definitive account concerning when and how the FAA gained situational awareness that each of the four commercial aircraft was hijacked by terrorists on the morning of 9/11, when and how the FAA notified the military about each of the hijacked aircraft, and when and how the military responded.

Unless otherwise noted, all times presented are rounded to the nearest minute. None of the audio excerpts in this document [was] derived from cockpit voice recorders. Where possible, individual names, phone numbers, excessive static noise, and excessive periods of "dead space" have been removed from the audio excerpts. Absolutely no content within the audio excerpts has been altered.

1. THE FAA AND NORAD

On 9/11 the defense of U.S. air space depended on close interaction between two federal agencies: the FAA and the North American Aerospace Defense Command (NORAD). The last hijacking that involved U.S. air traffic controllers, FAA management, and military coordination, had occurred in 1993. In order to understand how the two agencies interacted eight years later, we will review their missions, command—and—control structures, and working relationship on the morning of 9/11.

1.1 FAA Mission and Structure

As of September 11, 2001, the FAA was mandated by law to regulate the safety and security of civil aviation. The purpose of its prescribed air traffic control responsibilities [was], and remains, to minimize the risk of aircraft collisions while maximizing the capacity and efficiency of air transport. To carry out its mission, the FAA utilized 22 Air Route Traffic Control Centers, nearly 26,000 operational air traffic controllers, over 400 air traffic control towers, 195 terminal radar approach control facilities, and over 34,000 system elements for surveillance, communications, navigation and landing aids, and weather sensing.

The primary job of Air Traffic Controllers is to maintain mandatory minimum separation between aircraft. When an airplane takes off, it reports to controllers sitting in airport control tower facilities. At major metropolitan airports the tower controllers pass control quickly to short range (but higher resolution) radar control facilities known as Terminal Radar Approach Controls (TRACONs). Once an aircraft is approximately 30 miles from its point of departure, TRACON controllers "hand off" the aircraft and its transponder tracking signal to the corresponding Traffic Control Center whose airspace the aircraft will enter next.

These Traffic Control Centers are grouped together under seven regional facilities that help manage and oversee operations within their airspace. They also operate in close coordination with the Air Traffic Control System Command Center, commonly referred to as the "Command Center." The Command Center is located in Herndon, Virginia. Its primary responsibility is to oversee day – to – day operations within the entire airspace system, to keep traffic levels manageable for controllers working at the en – route centers.

In the FAA chain of command, the regional facilities report to FAA headquarters in Washington, DC. It is responsible for the management, operation and overall safety of the National Air System. A Washington Operations Center located at FAA headquarters receives notifications from the en route centers and the regions of incidents affecting the National Air System, including accidents and hijackings.

FAA Centers often receive information and make operational decisions independent of one another. On 9/11, the four hijacked aircraft were monitored mainly by four of these FAA Air Route Traffic Control Centers, 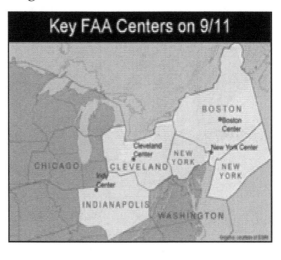 based in Boston, New York, Cleveland, and Indianapolis. Each Center thus had part of the knowledge of what was going on across the system. But it is important to remember that what Boston Center knew was not necessarily known by the Centers in New York, Cleveland, or Indianapolis.

Controllers track airliners like the four aircraft hijacked on 9/11 primarily by watching the data from a signal emitted by the aircraft's transponder equipment. The four aircraft hijacked on 9/11, like all aircraft traveling above 10,000 feet, were required to emit a unique transponder signal while in flight.

On 9/11, the terrorists turned off the transponders on three of the four hijacked aircraft. With the transponder turned off, it may be possible, although more difficult, to track an aircraft by its primary radar returns. A primary radar return occurs when the signal sent from a radar site bounces off an object in the sky and indicates the presence of that object. But primary radar returns do not include the transponder data, which show the aircraft's identity and altitude. Controllers at Centers rely on transponder signals and usually do not display primary radar returns on their scopes. But they can change the configuration of their radar scopes so they can see primary radar returns. In fact, the controllers did just that on 9/11 when the transponders were turned off in three of the four hijacked aircraft. Tower or terminal approach controllers handle a wider variety of lower—flying aircraft; they often use primary radar returns as well as transponder signals.

This overview of the FAA's organizational structure and how the FAA tracks aircraft within the NAS provides [part of] the framework for our findings concerning the operational facts of 9/11. The framework for a clear understanding of the operational facts is incomplete [,however,] without an overview of the command structure, mission and posture of NORAD as it existed on 9/11.

1.2 NORAD Mission and Structure

NORAD was, and is, responsible for the air defense of the continental United States. On 9/11, NORAD's air defense mission was to "destroy, nullify, or reduce the effectiveness of attacking enemy aircraft or missiles" by providing "Total Force Air Defense and threat warning to North America through readiness, detection and identification, and if necessary, force application."

To perform its air defense mission, NORAD consists of three regions: Alaskan NORAD Region (ANR), Canadian NORAD Region (CANR), and the Continental U.S. NORAD Region (CONR). CONR is further broken into three sectors: Western Air Defense Sector at McChord AFB, Wash.; Northeast Air Defense Sector at Rome, N.Y.; and Southeast Air Defense Sector at Tyndall AFB, Fla., which is also the headquarters for CONR. In the deployment of U.S. air defense assets, the Sectors report to CONR, and CONR reports to NORAD Headquarters, located in Colorado Springs, CO.

On 9/11, NORAD's continental U.S. (CONUS) air defense posture included 7 alert bases and 14 alert fighter aircraft. Each base had 2 fighter aircraft on alert. Alert aircraft were under the tactical control of the three regional sectors. NEADS, the sector that responded to all four hijacked aircraft on 9/11, had 2 alert bases and 4 alert fighter aircraft under [its] tactical control—two F-15s from the Otis Air National Guard Base in Cape Cop, Massachusetts and two F-16s from the Langley Air Force Base in Langley, Virginia.

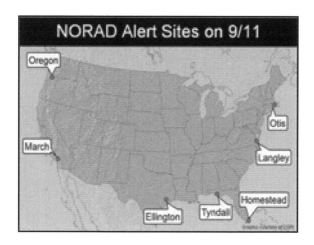

The key decisions in the nation's immediate air defense response to the 9/11 attacks were made by the military personnel at NEADS. NEADS conducts operations from a Sector Operations Command Center ("SOCC"). In normal day to day operations, the SOCC is led by a Mission Crew Commander ("MCC"). The MCC monitors the SOCC floor, receives reports from numerous watch—standers manning radar consoles, and makes tactical decisions based on those reports. Normally, the MCC also directs the updating of CONR and NORAD Headquarters through a secure computer terminal communication called a "chat log." During exercises or real—world operations, a Battle Commander assumes the highest authority at NEADS, oversees the MCC and the SOCC, and communicates directly with the Commander at CONR.

CONR is responsible for coordinating the sector commands and the air defense for CONUS. The CONR Region Commander is the highest ranking military authority at CONR, and reports to NORAD. On 9/11, the operations center at CONR was called the Regional

Air Operations Center (RAOC). The highest authority at CONR is the CONR Battle Commander (CONR BC). On 9/11, the RAOC floor, unlike sector operations centers, did not utilize radar scopes, or any direct—feed radar data from the FAA or NORAD radar sites. Instead, it used computer terminals to display manually entered tracks, and communicated with the Sectors by both secure and unsecure phone lines and various computer—based chat logs.

NORAD Headquarters (HQ)exercises command authority over NEADS via CONR. NORAD HQ operations are run from the Cheyenne Mountain Operations

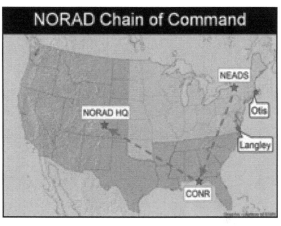

Center (CMOC) which is located in Cheyenne Mountain, Colorado. NORAD's Command Director runs the CMOC and is responsible for deciding the appropriate level of response from NORAD assets, and for communicating with the National Military Command Center (NMCC) which is located at the Pentagon. CMOC did not possess direct radar picture feeds from either FAA or NORAD radar facilities.

2. PROTOCOLS FOR RESPONDING TO HIJACKINGS

Before we proceed to the chronology of events of 9/11, we turn to a description of the protocols of both the FAA and NORAD for response to a hijacking event. As they existed on 9/11, the protocols for the FAA to obtain military assistance from NORAD required multiple levels of notification and approval at the highest levels of government before FAA and NEADS personnel would be authorized to communicate and coordinate an operational response.

Pre-9/11, FAA guidance to ATCs on hijack procedures was predicated on the assumption that the aircraft pilot would notify the controller of the hijack via radio communication or by "squawking" a Mode 3 transponder code of 7500 — the universal code for a hijack in progress.

FAA protocols in existence on 9/11 required ATCs to notify their supervisor when a hijacking occurred, or was believed to have occurred. Supervisors were then required to notify the managers of their facility and the corresponding ROC. The ROC facility was then required to notify the WOC at FAA Headquarters.

WOC duty officers were then required to notify the FAA's senior leadership, specifically the FAA "hijack coordinator" — identified as "the Director or his designate of the FAA Office of Civil Aviation Security." When FAA HQ receive[d] a report of a confirmed hijack, the FAA hijack coordinator on duty at HQ was required to make "direct contact" with the National Military Command Center located at the Pentagon and "request the military to provide an escort aircraft" to 1) "[a]ssure positive flight following"; 2) "[r]eport unusual observances"; and 3) "[a]id search and rescue in the event of an emergency." The NMCC would then seek and obtain approval from the Office of the Secretary of Defense (OSD) to provide military assistance.

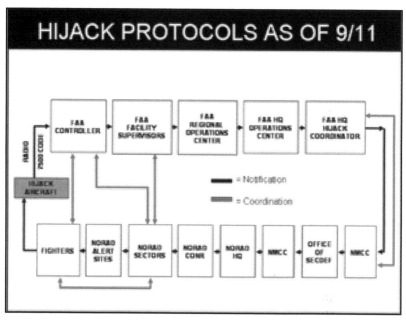

When approval for military assistance [was] granted by the OSD, the NMCC would contact the Commander-in-Chief ("CINC") NORAD in Colorado to advise NORAD that FAA's request for a fighter escort ha[d] been approved. NORAD HQ would then advise the NORAD region where the hijacked aircraft [was] located of the need to provide a fighter escort. If the hijacked aircraft [was] located in CONUS, as all 4 hijacked aircraft were on 9/11, NORAD officials would contact CONR in Panama City, Florida. CONR officials would then identify the appropriate NORAD Sector and assets that would be tasked to provide an operational response to the hijack event. If the hijacked aircraft was located in the northeast region of the United States, as all 4 hijacked aircraft were on 9/11, CONR would notify NEADS, in Rome, New York. NORAD HQ officials would then contact NMCC and identify NEADS as the defense sector tasked with the duty to provide a fighter escort for the hijacked aircraft.

The NMCC [would] then "advise the FAA hijack coordinator [of] the identification and location of the squadron tasked to provide escort aircraft." NMCC would finally "authorize direct coordination between FAA and the designated military unit." Upon completion of this approval process, the FAA en route center that [was] tracking the hijacked aircraft would be authorized to coordinate the military response with NEADS. In coordinating a timely response, the FAA facility would have to provide NEADS the following information 1) the call sign of the hijacked aircraft; 2) the time in universal time code; 3) the position of the hijacked aircraft in latitude and longitude; 4) the aircraft's heading; 5) the aircraft's speed; 6) the aircraft's altitude; and 7) if the fighter escort has been launched, its position with respect to the hijacked aircraft if requested by NEADS. If the hijacking event was within the coverage of NORAD's radar system, "every attempt" would be made to have the hijacked aircraft squawk 7500 to facilitate NEADS' ability to track the aircraft.

"Except when specifically directed otherwise by FAA headquarters," existing protocol provided the fighter escort aircraft must remain covert and be "vectored to a position five miles directly behind the hijacked aircraft." Indeed, on 9/11, the fighter aircraft, once scrambled and launched, were prepared and trained to: 1) approach and identify the target and 2) provide a covert escort (a "shadow") for the aircraft until it landed safely at an airport.

Clearly, the protocol in place on 9/11 for the FAA and NORAD to respond to a hijacking was extremely time intensive. When the clock began ticking with the first hijack of American 11 on the morning of 9/11, the time needed to follow the existing protocol would not be a luxury afforded anyone that day.

3. THE OPERATIONAL FACTS OF 9/11

Despite the multitude of news—paper and other media accounts, congressional and Commission testimony, and books and periodicals devoted to the government's response to the 9/11 attacks, the operational sequence that follows has never been told. Indeed, the facts of the morning of 9/11 directly contradict the official version of events, as presented publicly in testimony proffered before this Commission on May 23, 2003. Our chronology reveals the greatest amount of notice the military received of any of the 4 hijacked planes was the 9 minutes' notice NEADS received of the first hijacked aircraft, American 11, prior to it crashing into the North Tower of the World Trade Center at 8:46:40. NEADS received notice of the second hijacked plane, United 175, as it exploded into the South Tower of the World Trade Center at 9:03:02. NEADS received no notice that American 77 was hijacked (it received a report that the aircraft was missing, with no mention of its having been hijacked or of its location, three-to-five minutes before American 77 crashed into the Pentagon at 9:37:46). Finally, NEADS received notice that United 93 was hijacked at 10:07, four minutes after the flight had crashed in a field in Pennsylvania at 10:03:11.

	Notification Established by Commission Staff			Notification presented to Commission at May 2003 Hearing	
Flight	Impact	Time	Warning	Time	Warning
AA11	8:46:40	8:38	9 minutes	8:40	7 minutes
UA175	9:03:02	9:03	0 minutes	9:05	0 minutes
AA77	9:37:46	None	0 minutes	9:24	14 minutes
UA93	10:03:11	10:07	0 minutes	9:16	47 minutes

4.   AMERICAN 11

4.1   FAA Awareness

At 8:00 on September 11, 2001, American Airlines Flight 11 began its takeoff roll at Logan Airport in Boston. A Boeing 767, American 11 was bound for Los Angeles with 81 passengers and 11 crewmembers. By 8:09, American 11 had been passed from air traffic control at Logan Airport to Boston's regional en route center in Nashua, NH, some fifty miles from Boston. The Boston controller at the Boston Sector Radar Position directed the flight to "climb and maintain level two eight zero."

The controller followed this, at 8:10, with an instruction to "climb maintain flight level two niner zero," which was affirmed by American 11. At 8:13, the controller instructed the flight to "turn twenty degrees right," which the flight acknowledged: "twenty right American 11."

This was the last transmission to which the flight responded.

Sixteen seconds after receiving the acknowledgment from the pilot of the turn, the controller instructed the flight to "climb maintain level three five zero," an ultimate cruising altitude of 35,000 feet. When there was no response, the controller repeated the command ten seconds later, and then tried repeatedly to raise the flight.

According to the controller, at that point, he thought "maybe the pilots weren't paying attention, or there's something wrong with the frequency." He used the emergency frequency to try and [reach] the pilot. There was still no response." Indeed, numerous controllers interviewed at various FAA facilities stated it was a common occurrence prior to 9/11 to lose radio contact with pilots of commercial aircraft for a brief period of time. Controllers attributed the frequent losses of radio contact to electrical problems, pilot inattentiveness, failure to change frequencies and other examples unrelated to hijackings.

At this point—from 8:15 until 8:24 on the transcript—the Boston sector controller attempted to contact American 11 nine times, all unsuccessfully. At 8:21, American 11 changed course, heading northwest, and someone turned off the transponder. With a turned off transponder the information available to the controller was severely compromised: controllers could receive data on the plane's location, but could only loosely approximate its speed, had no way of knowing or even guessing its altitude, and could only identify it as a "primary radar target," not as a specific squawking flight.17 The controller "very quietly turned to the supervisor and said, `Would you please come over here? I think something is seriously wrong with this plane. I don't know what. It's either mechanical, electrical, I think, but I'm not sure.'" At this point, neither the controller nor his supervisor suspected hijacking. The supervisor instructed the controller to follow the standard operating procedures for the handling of a "no radio" (known as "NORDO") aircraft. Accordingly, the controller checked the working condition of his own equipment, then attempted to raise the flight on the 121.5 guard frequency. Boston Center controllers then tried to contact the airline to establish communication with the flight, and became more concerned when the flight began to move through the arrival route for Logan Airport, and then toward another sector's airspace.

About five minutes after the hijacking began, Flight Attendant Betty Ong contacted the American Airlines Southeastern Reservation Office in North Carolina to report an emergency aboard the flight. Following is a portion of the tape of that call.

The controllers moved "all the airplanes ... from Albany to New York to Syracuse, NY out of the way because that's the track he was going on," and searched from aircraft to aircraft on the company frequency in an effort to have another pilot contact American 11.

At 8:24:38, American 11 began a turn to the south and the following transmission came from American 11:

This Boston Sector controller heard something unintelligible over the radio, and did not hear the specific words "[w]e have some planes" at the time. The next transmission came seconds later:

The controller has told the media and Commission

staff during interviews, when he heard this second transmission, he "felt from those voices the terror" and immediately knew something was very wrong. He knew it was a hijack."

Controllers at Boston Center discussed attempts to contact American 11, the aircraft's altitude and whether someone had taken over the cockpit of the aircraft:

The controller alerted his supervisor to the threatening communication. The supervisor assigned a senior controller to assist the American 11 controller, and redoubled efforts to ascertain the flight's altitude. Because the initial transmission was not heard clearly, the Manager of Boston Center instructed the Center's Quality Assurance Specialist to "pull the tape" of the radio transmission, listen to it closely, and report on what he heard. Between 8:25 and 8:32, in accordance with the FAA protocol, Boston Center managers started notifying their chain of command that American 11 had been hijacked. At 8:28, Boston Center called the Command Center in Herndon, Virginia to advise management that it believed American 11 had been hijacked and was heading toward New York Center's airspace. By this point in time, American 11 had taken a dramatic turn to the south. Command Center immediately established a teleconference between Boston, New York and Cleveland Centers to allow Boston Center to provide situational awareness to the centers that adjoined Boston in the event the rogue aircraft entered their airspace.

The Command Center subsequently provided the following update on the situation to an unknown air traffic control facility:

At 8:32, the Command Center passed word of a possible hijacking to the Operations Center at FAA headquarters. The duty officer replied that security personnel at headquarters had just begun discussing the hijack situation on a conference call with the New England Regional office.

Also at 8:32, Michael Woodward of American Airlines took a call from Flight Attendant Madeline "Amy" Sweeney that lasted approximately twelve minutes. Although the call was not taped, Woodward's colleague, Nancy Wyatt, standing at his side, contacted Ray Howland in the American Airlines System Operations Center (SOC) to report the content of the ongoing call between Woodward and Amy Sweeney. Wyatt was able to relay information to the SOC as she heard Woodward's side of the conversation and read the notes he was taking. Following are two excerpts, which span several minutes, from the call to Howland.

At 8:34, as FAA headquarters received its initial notification that American 11 had been hijacked, the Boston sector controller received a third transmission from American 11.

In succeeding minutes, controllers in both Boston Center and New York Center attempted to ascertain the altitude of the southbound American 11.

Information about what was going on within American 11 started to get conveyed within the ATC system. At 8:40, Boston Center, through the Command Center, provided a report to New York TRACON on American 11. And at 8:43, a Command Center air traffic specialist warned Washington en route center that American 11 was a "possible hijack" and would be headed towards Washington Center's airspace if it continued on a southbound track.

American 11 crashed into the North Tower of the World Trade Center at 8:46:40. [Word of the crash of an airplane began to work its way quickly through the FAA's New York Center.]

4.2 Military Notification and Response

After Boston Center's managers notified the New England Region of the events concerning American 11, they did not wait for military assistance as notification was passed up the chain of command to FAA headquarters. In an attempt to get fighter aircraft airborne to track American 11, Boston Center's managers took the initiative and called a manager at the FAA Cape Cod facility at 8:34. They asked the Cape Cod manager to contact Otis Air Force Base in Cape Cod, Massachusetts to get fighters airborne to "tail" the hijacked aircraft.

Boston Center managers also tried to obtain assistance from a former alert site in Atlantic City, unaware that it had been phased out.

At 8:37:52, Boston Center's persistence finally paid dividends. They called the North American Aerospace Defense Command's (NORAD) Northeast Air Defense Sector (NEADS) and notified NEADS about the suspected hijacking of American 11.

The United States' military defense of its homeland on 9/11 began with this call. Indeed, this was the first notification received by the military—at any level—that American [11] had been hijacked. NEADS promptly ordered to battle stations the two F-15 alert aircraft at Otis Air Force Base, Massachusetts, about 153 miles away from New York City.

At NEADS, the reported hijack was relayed immediately to Battle Commander Colonel Robert Marr, who was stationed in the Battle Cab in preparation for a scheduled NORAD exercise. Col. Marr asked the same question—confirming that the hijacking was "real-world" —then ordered fighter pilots at Otis Air Force Base in Massachusetts to battle-stations.

He then phoned Maj. General Larry Arnold, commanding General of the First Air Force and CONR. Col. Marr advised him of the situation, and sought authorization to scramble the Otis fighters in response

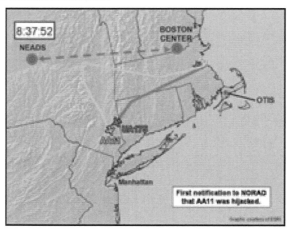

to the reported hijacking. General Arnold instructed Col. Marr "to go ahead and scramble the airplanes and we'd get permission later. And the reason for that is that the procedure ... if you follow the book, is they [law enforcement officials] go to the duty officer of the national military center, who in turn makes an inquiry to NORAD for the availability of fighters, who then gets permission from someone representing the Secretary of Defense. Once that is approved then we scramble an aircraft. We didn't wait for that."30 General Arnold then picked up the phone and talked to the operations deputy up at NORAD and said, "Yeah, we'll work with the National Military Command Center (NMCC). Go ahead and scramble the aircraft."

The scramble order was passed from the Battle Commander (BC) to the Mission Crew Commander (MCC), who passed the order to the Weapons Director (WD). Almost immediately, however, a problem arose. The Weapons Director asked: "MCC. I don't know where I'm scrambling these guys to. I need a direction, a destination." Because the hijackers had turned off the plane's transponder, the plane appeared only as a primary track on radar.

NEADS personnel spent the next minutes searching their radar scopes for the elusive primary radar track, as NEADS' Identification (ID) Technicians contacted the Military Operations Specialist (MOS) Desk (a civilian employee position at FAA Centers) at Boston Center in an effort to locate the aircraft:

F-15 fighters were ordered scrambled at 8:46 from Otis Air Force Base and vectored toward military airspace off the coast of Long Island.

As the order to scramble Otis fighters came at 8:46, American 11 was hitting the World Trade Center and United 175 was being hijacked in New York Center's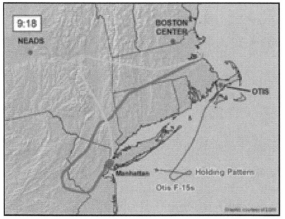

airspace. The military did not hear anything about United 175 until it crashed into the South Tower of the World Trade Center.

Working over the phone with the FAA Center in Boston, at least one NEADS tracker found a primary track roughly eight miles east-northeast of Manhattan, but the track faded before he could confirm it with Boston Center. Unbeknownst to the military, the Otis fighters were scrambled [at] nearly the exact time that American 11 crashed into the North Tower. Radar data show the Otis fighters were airborne at 8:53.

The Mission Crew Commander explained to the Battle Cab the plan:

Shortly after 8:50, while NEADS personnel struggled to locate American 11, word reached the floor that a plane had hit the World Trade Center.

The initial reaction of the Mission Crew Commander was to send the fighters directly to New York in response to the news of the crash. Upon being advised, however, that the quickest route would be to bring the fighters out away from the New York area traffic, the decision was made to bring the fighters down to military air space and to "hold as needed."

4.3 Commission Findings and Assessment

The interplay at the operational levels of the FAA and NORAD regarding American 11 is notable in several respects. First, and most important, Boston Center and NEADS took immediate actions to facilitate a quicker response than a strict following of the official protocols would have allowed for. Boston Center elected to request assistance directly from the Northeast Air Defense Sector.

When the request reached NEADS, the Battle Commander and the CONR Commander, rather than seeking authorization to scramble aircraft through the chain of command and, ultimately, the Secretary of Defense, chose to authorize the action on their own and, as General Arnold (CONR Commander) put it, "seek the authorities later." It is difficult to fault either decision. Given the emergent nature of the situation, the reports of "trouble in the cockpit," and the fact that there was no easily identified transponder signal emitted from the aircraft, the necessity to shortcut the hijack protocols seems apparent. It is clear, moreover, that the protocols themselves were ill-suited to the American 11 event; the multi-layered notification and approval process assumed a "classic" hijack scenario in which there is ample time for notice to occur, there is no difficulty in locating the aircraft, the hijackers intend to land the aircraft somewhere, and the military's role is limited to identification and escort of the aircraft. Indeed, the hijack protocols were not reasserted on 9/11 until the attacks were completed.

However, bypassing the established protocols for air emergencies, though justified in the case of American 11, may have had an unintended ill effect as the day wore on; leadership at the national levels at the FAA and DOD [was] not involved – or [was] involved only after the fact – in the critical decision making and the evolving situational awareness regarding American 11. As the Commission has presented in its June 2004 public hearing and in the official "9/11 Commission Report," they [national leaders] would remain largely irrelevant to the critical decision making and unaware of the evolving situation "on the ground" until the attacks were completed.

The critical information NEADS received would continue to come from Boston Center, which relayed information as it was overheard on FAA teleconferences. Indeed, at one point that morning the Mission Crew Commander, in the absence of regular communication from anyone else at FAA, encouraged the Military position at Boston Center to continue to provide information: "if you get anything, if you—any of your controllers see anything that looks kind of squirrelly, just give us a yell. We'll get those fighters in that location."39 The NEADS ID Technicians would complain repeatedly that morning: "Washington has no clue what the hell is going on Washington has no clue."

The Boston Military FAA representative, when interviewed, expressed astonishment that he had been the principal source of information for the NEADS personnel on the morning of 9/11; he stated his belief that he must have been one of several FAA sources constantly updating NEADS that morning. No open line was established between NEADS and CONR and either FAA headquarters or the Command Center at Herndon until the attacks were virtually over.

It is clear that, as the order to scramble came at 8:46, just as American 11 was hitting the World Trade Center, the military had insufficient notice of the hijacking to position its assets to respond. This reality would also be repeated throughout the morning. Indeed, the eight minutes' notice that NEADS had of American 11 would prove to be the most notice the sector would receive that morning of any of the hijackings, and the sector's inability to locate the primary radar track until the last few readings would also recur.

5. UNITED 175

5.1 FAA Awareness

United Airlines Flight 175, a Boeing 767 carrying 65 passengers en route from Boston's Logan Airport to Los Angeles, took off from Logan Airport at 8:14, and made contact with the Boston Air Route Traffic Control Center at 8:19. Five minutes later, the flight was cleared to a cruising altitude of 31,000 feet.

At 8:37, the Kingston sector controller asked the pilots of United 175, among other flights, to look for American 11.

The controller then turned United 175 thirty degrees to the right away from American 11.

The controller explained to Commission staff that he turned United 175 and directed the flight to maintain an altitude of 31,000 feet because of the unpredictable behavior of American 11.

United 175 was then passed to the New York Air Traffic Control Center at Ronkonkoma, NY, reporting in at 8:40. The controller acknowledged United 175, then, like the Boston Center controller, engaged US Air Flight 583 in a discussion about American 11, asking whether Boston Center had asked the pilot to locate American 11. The pilot of US Air 583 responded affirmatively and gave an estimation of 29,000 feet for the altitude of American 11. The controller noted that "it looks like they shut off their transponder that's why the question about [where it is]." At this point, at approximately 8:42, the pilot of United 175 broke in with the following transmission:

The controller turned United 175 away from the aircraft (American 11) as a safety precaution. At this point,

United 175 had entered New York Center's airspace and unfortunately, the controller responsible for United 175 was the same controller assigned the job of tracking the hijacked American 11. At 8:47, nearly simultaneously with the impact of American 11 into the World Trade Center, United 175's assigned transponder code changed from 1470 to 3020, and then again to 3321. These changes were not noticed, however, for several minutes, as the controller was focused on trying to determine the location of American 11, which had disappeared as a primary radar track. Indeed, New York Center was completely focused on the situation with American 11, as indicated in the following report given by New York Center on a teleconference that had been established between their center, Boston Center and the Command Center. (Note that this report was made at approximately 8:48, just minutes after the impact of American 11 into the North Tower, though that was not known by the individual at the time).

Delta Airlines Flight 1489 radioed in at 8:50 and advised the same controller there was "a lot of smoke in lower Manhattan" and the World Trade Center looked like it was on fire. The controller acknowledged the message at 8:51, and agreed to pass on any news, then noticed a change in the transponder reading from United 175. The controller asked United 175 to recycle its transponder to the proper code. There was no response.

At 8:52, the controller made repeated attempts to reach the crew of United 175. Still, there was no response.

At 8:53, after several unsuccessful attempts to reach United 175, the controller contacted another peer to discuss the situation.

The controller explained to Commission staff that he became alarmed when he saw a change of altitude along with the change in the transponder frequency; prior to the change in altitude, he assumed that the change in transponder frequency was human or mechanical error. US Air Flight 583 then radioed in and said he was getting "reports over the radio of a commuter plane hitting the World Trade Center". The controller spent the next several minutes handing off the other flights on his scope to other controllers and moving aircraft out of the way of the unidentified aircraft (believed to be United 175) as it moved southwest and then turned northeast toward New York City.

At approximately 8:55, the controller-in-charge notified the Operations Manager that she believed United 175 had also been hijacked. During interviews with Commission staff, the Air Traffic Manager (ATM) for New York Center said he made more than one attempt to notify the FAA Eastern Region Offices that United 175 may be a hijacked aircraft but was told by a staffer there that the managers were discussing a hijacked aircraft (presumably American 11) and refused to be disturbed. At 8:58, the New York Center controller searching for United 175 told another New York controller "we might have a hijack over here, two of them."

Between 9:01 and 9:02, a manager from New York Center told the FAA Command Center, in Herndon, VA:

The other situation New York Center referred to was United 175. The evidence suggests this conversation was the only notice received prior to the second crash by either FAA HQ or Command Center that there was a second hijack.

While the Command Center was told about this "other aircraft" at 9:01, New York Center contacted New York terminal approach control and asked for help in locating United 175.

The controllers observed the plane in a rapid descent; the radar data terminated over lower Manhattan. At 9:03:02, United 175 crashed into World Trade Center's South Tower.

As United 175 was about to strike the South Tower, in a conversation monitored by FAA Command Center, a manager from Boston Center confirmed what was said by the hijackers on board American 11 during the first radio transmission:

After the impact into the South Tower, Boston Center updated the FAA's New England Region:

Boston Center immediately advised the New England Region that it was going to stop all aircraft scheduled to depart from any airport within Boston Center.

At 9:05, Boston Center confirmed for both FAA Command Center and New England Region that the hijackers aboard American 11 said "we have planes."

At exactly the same time that the "we have planes" was confirmed, both Boston Center and New York Center closed down their airspace. The result of this action was that aircraft were not permitted to depart from, arrive at, or travel through those Centers' airspace until further notice.

After the second WTC crash, the Boston Center Operations Manager feared there may be additional attacks. He asked a New England Regional security representative if warnings could be sent to airborne aircraft by the airlines via a text messaging system (ACARS).

Within minutes of the second impact at the World Trade Center, Boston Center's Operations Manager instructed all air traffic controllers in his center to use the radio frequencies to inform all aircraft in Boston Center of the events unfolding in New York and to advise the aircraft to heighten cockpit security in light of those events. Her[e] are several examples of the cautionary radio transmissions sent by ZBW to other aircraft:

At approximately 9:15, another Boston Center Manager ask[ed] Command Center to relay the message to all FAA centers in the country to use heightened cockpit security:

Commission staff has found no evidence to suggest that Command Center mangers acted on Boston's request to issue a nationwide alert to aircraft. One Command Center manager interviewed told Commission staff that the FAA mindset on 9/11 was such that they would never have relayed this message directly to all pilots. She said the FAA would pass situational awareness to the airline company representatives who, in turn, would determine if such action was necessary.

5.2 Military Notification and Response

The first indication that the NEADS air defenders had of the second hijacked aircraft, United 175, came in a phone call from New York Center at 9:03.

The ID Technicians were on the phone with Boston Center seeking further information on United 175 when they found out that the plane may have crashed. Before retrieving the flight's vital statistics for NEADS, Boston Center confirmed the second crash at the Trade Center. There had been no prior notification that the plane was hijacked, or, for that matter, missing. The fighters from Otis Air Force Base were south of Long Island at the time.

The Mission Crew Commander's reaction to the second explosion at the World Trade Center was to reject the idea of holding the fighters in military air space away from Manhattan.

The FAA cleared the air space. Radar data show that at 9:13, when the Otis fighters were about 115 miles away from the city, the fighters exited their holding pattern and set a course direct for Manhattan. They arrived at 9:25 and established a combat air patrol (CAP) over the city.

Because the Otis fighters had expended a great deal of fuel in flying first to military air space and then to New York, the battle commanders were concerned about refueling. As NEADS personnel looked for refueling tankers in the vicinity of New York, the Mission Crew Commander considered scrambling the Langley fighters to New York to provide back-up for the Otis fighters until the NEADS Battle Cab ordered "[b]attle stations only at Langley."

The alert fighters at Langley Air Force Base were ordered to battle stations at 9:09.

Col. Marr, the battle commander at NEADS, and General Arnold, the CONR Commander, both recall that the planes were held on battle stations, as opposed to scrambling, because they might be called upon to relieve the Otis fighters over New York City if a refueling tanker was not located, and also because of the general uncertainty of the situation in the sky. According to retired Col. William Scott at the Commission's May 23, 2003 hearing, "At 9:09, Langley F-16s are directed to battle stations, just based on the general situation and the breaking news, and the general developing feeling about what's going on." NORAD had no indication that any other plane had been hijacked.

5.3 Commission Findings and Assessment

The most noteworthy aspect of the time sequence recounted above is a time that is not mentioned: 8:43. In the days immediately following 9/11, both NORAD and FAA identified 8:43 as the time at which NORAD was notified of the hijacking of United 175; this time was picked up by The Washington Post and other prominent media outlets, and widely disseminated in the public record. The tapes and transcripts, corroborated by witness interviews, show, however, that 8:43 could not have been the time of notification. The FAA controller did not notice the change in transponder signal from United 175 until 8:51; there is no way that FAA could have notified NORAD of the hijacking at 8:43 when it did not even realize there was a problem with the flight until eight minutes later.

The Commission has been unable to identify the source of the inaccurate 8:43 hijack notification time for United 175. Both FAA and NORAD, however, eventually dropped that notification time from their official version of events; neither can account for its original inclusion.

The inclusion of an 8:43 notification time in the early press releases from FAA and NORAD muddied the public record by raising questions about whether the Otis fighters were vectored properly; a flight path into military air space is difficult to justify when there is a reported second hijacking and one aircraft has already crashed into the World Trade Center. The actual flight path taken by the fighters is defensible given the fact that the second hijacking was reported as it was concluding; the Mission Crew Commander wanted the fighters eventually over New York City, but in the absence of a second emergent event was willing to hold the fighters over military airspace until the FAA could clear a path.

6. AMERICAN 77

6.1 FAA Awareness

American Airlines Flight 77 began its takeoff roll from Dulles International Airport at 8:20. The flight proceeded normally through air space controlled by the Washington Air Traffic Control Center, and was handed off to Indianapolis Center at approximately 8:40, with which it made routine radio contact.

American 77 was acknowledged by the controller, who had fourteen other planes in his sector at the time, and later instructed American 77 to climb to thirty-five thousand feet and to turn right ten degrees. At 8:51, American 77 acknowledged the clearance it was given to navigate direct to the Falmouth navigational aid. This was the last transmission from American 77.

At 8:54, the flight began a left turn towards the south without authorization. Shortly after it began the turn, the aircraft was observed descending. At 8:56, as the plane continued to deviate slightly to the south from its flight plan, it was lost from radar completely; the transponder signal was gone, and the plane also disappeared as a primary radar target.

The controller tracking American 77 told the Commission he first noticed the aircraft turning to the southwest, and then saw the data disappear. The controller looked for primary radar returns. He searched along its projected flight path and the airspace to the southwest where it had started to turn. No primary targets appeared. He tried the radios, first calling the aircraft directly, then the airline. Again there was nothing. At this point, the Indianapolis controller had no knowledge of the situation in New York. He did not know that other aircraft had been hijacked. He believed American 77 had experienced serious electrical and/or mechanical failure, and was gone.

In addition, the controller reached out to controllers in other sectors at Indianapolis Center to advise them of the situation. The controllers agreed to "sterilize the air space" along the flight's projected westerly route so that other planes would not be affected by American 77. At 8:59, Indianapolis Center began to work with controllers in other centers to protect the airspace of American 77's projected flight path to the west.

After several minutes of searching, Indianapolis controllers once again contacted the airline:

At 9:08, the Indianapolis Center's Operations Manager requested the Traffic Management Unit to notify Air Force Search and Rescue in Langley, Virginia, of a possible crash of American 77. The Operations Manager also contacted the West Virginia State Police to advise them of the missing aircraft and ask whether they had any reports of a downed aircraft. At 9:09, Indianapolis Center reported to the Great Lakes Regional Operations Center a possible aircraft accident involving American 77 because of the simultaneous loss of radio communications and all radar contact. The Great Lakes Regional Operations Center passed this information along to FAA Headquarters at 9:24.

By 9:20, Indianapolis Center learned that there were other hijacked aircraft in the system, and began to doubt their initial assumption that American 77 had crashed. A discussion of this concern between the manager at Indianapolis and the Command Center in Herndon prompted the [delete: notified] Command Center to notify some FAA field facilities that American 77 was lost. By 9:21, the Command Center, some FAA field facilities, and American Airlines had started to search for American 77. They feared it had been hijacked. At 9:25, the Command Center advised FAA headquarters that American 77 was lost in Indianapolis Center's airspace, [and] that Indianapolis Center had no primary radar track and was looking for the aircraft.

The failure to find a primary radar return for American 77 led us to investigate this issue further. Radar reconstructions performed after 9/11 reveal that FAA radar equipment tracked the flight from the moment its transponder was turned off at 8:56. But for 8 minutes and 13 seconds, between 8:56 and 9:05, this primary radar information on American 77 was not displayed to controllers at Indianapolis Center. The reasons are technical, arising from the way the software processed radar information, as well as from poor primary radar coverage where American 77 was flying.

According to the radar reconstruction, American 77 re-emerged as a primary target on Indianapolis Center radar scopes at 9:05, east of its last known position. The target remained in Indianapolis Center's airspace for another six minutes, then crossed into the western portion of Washington Center's airspace at 9:10. As Indianapolis Center continued searching for the aircraft, two managers and the controller responsible for American 77 looked to the west and southwest along the flight's projected path, not east—where the aircraft was now heading. The managers did not instruct other controllers at Indianapolis Center to turn on their primary radar coverage to join in the search for American 77.

In sum, Indianapolis Center never saw American 77 turnaround. By the time it reappeared in primary radar coverage, controllers had either stopped looking for the aircraft 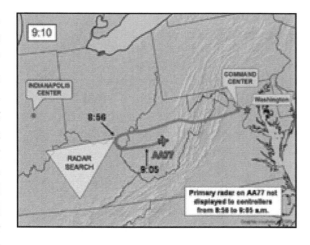 because they thought it had crashed or were looking toward the west. In addition, while the Command Center learned American 77 was missing, neither it nor FAA headquarters issued an "all points bulletin" to surrounding centers to search for primary radar targets. American 77 traveled undetected for 36 minutes on a course heading due east for Washington, DC.

6.2 Confusion Concerning the Fate of American 77

While Indianapolis Center was busy looking for American 77 to the west, some American Airlines' representatives believed that American 77 might have hit the World Trade Center. In an ensuing conversation with the FAA Command Center about the status of American 11, an American Airlines representative mentioned that American 77 was lost.

Even later, after 9:30, confusion surrounding American 77 still existed within at least some levels of the FAA:

American Airlines' notification to the FAA Command Center that American 77 was lost prompted Command Center representatives to call Indianapolis Center and seek further information on the aircraft:

That conversation led Command Center to notify some FAA field facilities that American 77 was lost and could not be located on radar. By no later than 9:21, FAA's Command Center in Herndon, some FAA field facilities and American Airlines had started to search for American 77 and feared it had been hijacked. Four minutes later, at 9:25, Command Center reported to FAA Headquarters all the information Command Center had learned regarding American 77.

As previously stated, American 77 disappeared from radar at 8:56. By no later than 9:18, FAA centers in Indianapolis, Cleveland, and Washington were aware that American 77 was missing and two aircraft had struck the World Trade Center. By 9:15, Air Force Search and Rescue was notified of the missing plane. At 9:24, Great Lakes Regional Operations Center notified the Washington Operations Center of the simultaneous loss of radio and radar contact with American 77. FAA Headquarters was aware American 77 was lost somewhere in the NAS.

By no later than 9:25, FAA's Herndon Command Center and FAA headquarters knew that two aircraft had crashed into the World Trade Center. They knew American 77 was lost. At least some FAA officials in Boston Center and the New England Region knew that a hijacker on board American 11 said "we have some planes." Concerns over the safety of other aircraft began to mount. A manager from

Command Center specifically asked FAA Headquarters if they wanted to order a "nationwide ground stop." While executives at FAA headquarters discussed the issuance of a national ground stop, at 9:25, Command Center exercised initiative and ordered all aircraft in the United States not to depart from any airports until further notice. Command Center's National Operations Manager, Ben Sliney, told the Commission that he gave this order based on his belief the attacks would continue, concern that the FAA could not locate American 77 and reports that other commercial aircraft may have been hijacked. Sliney said he believed he possessed the authority to issue this order and ordered the ground stop in an attempt to mitigate any potential further damage.

While Command Center prevented any aircraft from entering the NAS, they also continued their efforts to locate American 77. At 9:21, FAA Command Center advised a supervisor at Dulles Tracon that the FAA had lost contact with American 77 and was trying to find the aircraft. At 9:21, controllers at Dulles Tracon were advised by the FAA Command Center that a commercial aircraft was missing and instructed to look for primary targets. At 9:32 they found one. Several of the Dulles controllers "observed a primary target tracking eastbound at a high rate of speed" and notified Reagan National Airport. FAA personnel at both Reagan National and Dulles Airports notified the Secret Service. The identity or aircraft type was unknown at the time. This track was later confirmed to be American 77.

Just minutes before impact of American 77, Reagan Airport controllers vectored an unarmed National Guard C-130H cargo aircraft, which had just taken off en route to

Minnesota, to identify and follow the suspicious aircraft that Dulles Tracon had pointed out to them. The cargo aircraft attempted to follow the path of the unidentified aircraft, and at 9:38, seconds after impact, reported to the control tower that the aircraft crashed into the Pentagon.

6.3 Military Notification and Response

By no later than 9:21, FAA's Command Center in Herndon, some FAA field facilities and American Airlines had started to search for American 77 and feared it had been hijacked. Four minutes later, at 9:25, Command Center reported to FAA Headquarters all the information Command Center had learned regarding American 77. The military was completely unaware the search for American 77 had begun. In fact, the military would hear once again about American 11, a plane that had already crashed, before they received any notification that American 77 was lost.

At 9:21, the military officer at Boston Center, who had been listening in on a FAA teleconference run by FAA HQ in Washington, called the NEADS ID Technician Unit:

The mention of a "third aircraft" was not a reference to American 77. The report that American 11 was still airborne and heading toward Washington, DC was relayed immediately from the Mission Crew Commander to the Battle Cab. After consulting with the Battle Commander, the MCC issued the order, at 9:23, to scramble the Langley fighters in response to American 11.

The scramble order was processed and transmitted to Langley Air Force Base at 9:24. Shortly thereafter, NEADS commanders cancelled the "tail chase" using the Otis fighters since pursuing the plane from behind would leave New York airspace unprotected. Instead, the heading of the Langley fighters would be adjusted to send them to the Baltimore area. When interviewed by Commission staff, the Mission Crew Commander explained that the purpose of this change in strategy was to continue to protect New York air space, and to vector the fighters from Langley to come between the southbound aircraft and the nation's capital. Radar data show the Langley fighters airborne at 9:30.

Based on the mistaken report that American 11 was heading towards Washington, DC, NEADS personnel were actively seeking more information to assist in their search for the aircraft:

The military's situational awareness was summarized on the NEADS floor at 9:27, immediately after the Langley scramble, as follows: "Three planes unaccounted for. American Airlines 11 may still be airborne but the flight that — United 175 to the World Trade Center. We're not sure who the other one is."

On the floor at NEADS, the ID Technicians continued to attempt to locate American 11 after the Langley fighters were airborne. At the suggestion of the Boston Center Military Officer, the ID Technicians contacted Washington Center to ask whether they had located American 11. In that conversation, NEADS was told that Washington Center knew nothing about American 11 heading south. The NEADS ID Technicians then spoke with the Operations Manager at Washington Center:

This discussion was the first notice to the military that American 77 was missing, and it had come by chance. The time was 9:34. If NEADS had not placed that call to Washington Center, the NEADS air defenders would have received no information whatsoever that American 77 was even missing, although the FAA had been searching for it. No one at FAA headquarters ever asked for military assistance with American 77.

At 9:36, the FAA's Boston Center called NEADS and relayed the discovery about an aircraft closing in on Washington, an aircraft that still had not been linked with the missing American 77.

When pressed on whether the flight was in fact a deviating aircraft, Boston Center insisted that NEADS call Washington Center, which is where the aircraft was located and could actually be seen on radar. At 9:39, just moments after the impact at the Pentagon, Washington Center disclaimed any knowledge of the plane near the White House.

It is fair to infer, from Washington Center's complete lack of knowledge concerning the aircraft approaching the White House, that Boston Center received the 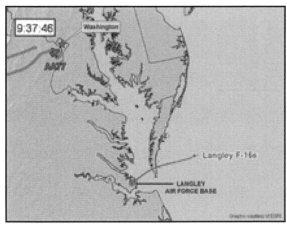 information about the aircraft from FAA headquarters. The startling information that a deviating aircraft was in close proximity to the White House prompted the Mission Crew Commander to order "AFIO" (Authorization for Interceptor Operations), which entailed taking immediate control of the Langley fighters from the FAA and responsibility for the safe flight path of the Langley fighters.

The Langley fighters were ordered to proceed directly to Washington, DC. The MCC then discovered, to his surprise, that the Langley fighters were not headed north toward the Baltimore area as previously instructed, but east over the ocean.

A combination of three factors explains why the Langley fighters initially traveled so far to the east, when their initial scramble order directed them on a heading to the north.

First, the Langley scramble order did not convey complete instructions. It instructed the fighters to "Scramble immediately time 1324... Scramble on a heading of 010 flight level 290."

Though the order did include a direction to fly — "010" and a flight altitude — 29,000 feet — it did not include a distance to the target, nor the target's location, two key components that are normally included in a scramble order. Indeed, NEADS did not know the location of the mistakenly reported southbound American 11 — at the time, there was no discernable target.

Second, a "generic" flight plan assigned to the Langley fighters incorrectly led them to believe that they were being ordered to fly due east (090) for 60 miles. In order to launch aircraft, the Langley AFB Tower was required to file an automated flight plan specifically designating the direction and distance of intended flight. Prior to 9/11, the standard — or generic — flight plan for aircraft departing Langley AFB to the east was "090 for 60" — meaning head 90 degrees (due east) for 60 miles. The generic "090 for

60" flight plan was utilized to expeditiously get aircraft airborne and out of the base's airspace. Langley Tower personnel assumed that once fighters got airborne they would be vectored to the target of interest by either NEADS or the FAA.

Third, both the lead Langley pilot and the FAA's Norfolk TRACON facility — which was briefly controlling the aircraft once it departed the Langley AFB airspace — assumed the flight plan instruction to go "090 for 60" was newer guidance that superceded [sic] the original scramble order instructions. In fact, shortly after the fighters got airborne, the lead Langley pilot was asked by Norfolk TRACON in what direction he wanted to head After brief discussion between the lead pilot (identified as "Quit 25") and Norfolk TRACON, it was mutually decided that the fighters would follow the flight plan guidance.

Put simply, the Langley pilots received flight direction guidance from both the scramble order and the Langley AFB departure flight plan, and continued on the latter heading for several minutes until a direction and geographic destination was provided.

Back at NEADS, controllers on the floor located an unknown primary radar track, but "it kind of faded" over Washington. The time was 9:38. The Pentagon had been struck by American 77 at 9:37:46. The Langley fighters were approximately 150 miles away.

6.4 Commission Findings and Assessment

The sequence outlined above is again noteworthy for its omission of notification times that have been widely circulated. In the official NORAD version of the events of 9/11, as presented to the Commission in May 2003, at 9:16, NORAD was notified that United 93 was a possible hijack and that notification was followed, at 9:24, by the notification that American 77 was a hijacked aircraft. According to retired Col. William Scott at the Commission's May 23, 2003 hearing, the FAA notified NORAD of the hijacking of United 93 at 9:16 (forty-five minutes prior to crash), and of the hijacking of American 77 at 9:24 (14 minutes prior to crash). Retired Col. Scott also indicated that the fighters at Langley Air Force Base were scrambled at 9:25 to meet the threat to Washington posed by American 77.

Retired General Larry Arnold amplified this information in testimony before the Commission, stating: "9:24 was the first time that we had been advised of American 77 as a possible hijacked airplane. Our focus — you have got to remember that there's a lot of other things going on simultaneously here — was on United 93, which was being pointed out to us very aggressively I might say by the FAA. We were advised [American 77] was possibly hijacked. And we had launched almost simultaneously with that, we launched the aircraft out of Langley to put them over top of Washington, DC, not in response to American Airlines 77, but really to put them in position in case United 93 were to head that way."

Based on its review of the tapes, transcripts and other records obtained under subpoena, as corroborated by witness interviews at NEADS, Commission staff can state unequivocally that the timeline and testimony presented at the Commission's May 23, 2003 hearing were not true. The 9:24 notification time for American 77 (as well as the claimed 9:16 notification for United 93) was inaccurately derived from a handwritten log maintained by the staff working for the Mission Crew Commander (the operational commander on watch). Called the "MCC/T Log," it was the principal log of events kept at NEADS on 9/11. At 9:24, the log records: "American Airlines #N334AA hijacked." This tail number refers not to American 77 but to American 11, the first hijacked aircraft. The subpoenaed tapes confirm that this time corresponds to the receipt of the tail number information on American 11 and to reports that American 11 was still airborne and headed towards Washington, DC.

Nor were the Langley fighters scrambled to meet the threat posed by American 77. The first notification to the military (NEADS) that American 77 is missing (there is no mention of it being hijacked at this point) comes at 9:34, ten minutes after the scramble has already been ordered at Langley Air Force Base.

The Langley fighters were initially scrambled not because of United 93, which had not been hijacked, nor because of American 77, which had not been reported to NEADS, but because of the mistaken report that American 11 had in fact not hit the World Trade Center, but was heading south towards Washington, DC. The fighters were ordered scrambled initially toward New York, and then vectored toward Baltimore, in an effort to intercept that mistakenly reported aircraft. The best evidence for both this false report and the resulting scramble is the subpoenaed NEADS tape, quoted above, which records the Mission Crew Commander's immediate reaction to the report: "Okay. American Airlines is still airborne, 11, the first guy. He's headed towards Washington, okay? I think we need to scramble Langley right now, and I'm going to—I'm going to take the fighters from Otis and try to chase this guy down if I can find him." Seconds after that reaction, the Mission Crew Commander ordered the scramble of the Langley fighters. This report of American 11 heading south—the cause of the Langley scramble—is reflected not just in taped conversations at NEADS, but in taped conversations at FAA centers, on chat logs compiled at NEADS, CONR, and NORAD, and in records extending to the highest levels of the federal government. The false report was also readily acknowledged in interviews of operational personnel. Nonetheless, it is not recounted in a single public timeline issued by FAA or DOD, nor in a single public statement by government officials. Instead, the scramble at Langley is attributed to the reported hijacking of American 77, United 93, or some combination of the two.

When interviewed, Col. Marr stated that he had discounted the report that American 11 was still airborne, and insisted that the Langley scramble was in response to "everything else that was going on" that morning, and referred specifically to United 93. When informed that United 93 had not been hijacked by the time of the Langley scramble, and that American 77 was not reported missing to the NEADS air defenders until after the Langley scramble had occurred, Col. Marr was unable to point to any other complicating factors that might have led to the Langley scramble.

Col. Marr's recollection is belied by the tapes and transcripts from the morning of 9/11, the testimony of his subordinates, and the contemporaneous records from the day. The Mission Crew Commander and the ID Technicians who were on duty that morning had no doubt that the sequence revealed on the tapes, in which the Mission Crew Commander orders Langley scrambled in immediate response to the news that American 11 is still airborne, was in fact what occurred.

The Commission has been unable to identify the source of the mistaken information regarding American 11. The Boston Center Military Desk person who provided the information to NEADS had been listening in on an FAA teleconference out of Washington, DC. A Senior FAA official who was working at Headquarters that morning recalls having passed the information to others, but does not know its source.

What is clear is that the introduction of a third hijacking into the FAA system proved to be extremely confusing, raising doubts as to the identities of the two planes that had crashed into the World Trade Center and leading, ultimately, to the false report that one of the original hijacked aircraft was still airborne, heading for Washington.

Overall, this sequence of events regarding American 77 again belies NORAD's official timeline and the testimony given at the Commission's May 23, 2003 hearing. Notification of American 77 as a missing aircraft came at 9:34, after the Langley fighters had already taken off. Remarkably, the notification, when it occurred, came completely fortuitously, not as the result of existing notification protocols between FAA and NORAD. The ID Technician at NEADS called Washington Center at the prompting of the Boston FAA Military desk, in order to find further information about American 11. If NEADS had not placed that call themselves, the NEADS air defenders would have received no notification whatsoever that American 77 was missing prior to its crash. Given the facts that there had already been two suicide hijackings and that the FAA—both at the Command Center and at several regional centers—had been searching for American 77 for over thirty minutes, the failure of FAA proactively to notify NORAD of the missing aircraft seems egregious, even in hindsight.

Even when FAA controllers at Dulles Tower did pick up the primary radar track of an unknown aircraft southwest of Washington, no one at FAA thought ask for military assistance. Once again, the NEADS air defenders received word of the unknown target from Boston Center's Military position, which happened to overhear the discussion of the sighting on a teleconference originating from Washington

7.   ANOTHER MISTAKEN REPORT: DELTA
     FLIGHT 1989

Right after the Pentagon was hit, NEADS learned of another possible hijacked aircraft. It was an aircraft that in fact had not been hijacked at all. After the second World Trade Center crash, Boston Center managers recognized that both aircraft were transcontinental 767 jetliners that had departed Logan Airport. Remembering the "we have some planes" remark, Boston Center guessed that Delta 1989 might also be hijacked. Boston Center called NEADS at 9:41 and identified Delta 1989; a 767 jet that had left Logan Airport for Las Vegas, as a possible hijack.

Because Delta 1989 had not turned off its transponder, NEADS never lost track of the aircraft as it moved west, reversed course over Toledo, headed east, and landed in Cleveland. NEADS even ordered fighter aircraft from Ohio and Michigan to intercept Delta 1989.

After receiving the initial report from Boston Center,

the NEADS ID Technicians called several FAA facilities to share the information they had learned about Delta 1989:

The ID Technician advised that all of their fighters had been scrambled on the New York and Washington events, and that NEADS was looking for other fighters to scramble to intercept the Delta flight.

At approximately 9:45, while one NEADS ID technician was confirming 1989 as a hijack to Cleveland Center, another ID Technician received a call from the Boston Center Military position advising that Delta 1989 might not be a hijack after all:

NEADS informed Boston Center that they were tracking Delta 1989 as it passed over Toledo. The NEADS air defenders continued to track Delta 1989 for the next several minutes, watching its every move until it landed in Cleveland.

The Mission Crew Commander, with his full complement of alert aircraft capping New York City and heading for Washington, decided to look for non-NORAD aircraft from the midwest to intercept the Delta flight. NEADS personnel contacted Toledo and Selfridge Air Force Bases and diverted fighters from training missions to intercept Delta 1989.

Just before 10:00, the Mission Crew Commander made the following report:

The Mission Crew Commander was advised, at approximately 10:00, that there was no authority to shoot the plane down; the rules of engagement only authorized NEADS to direct fighter aircraft to intercept, identify, and escort other aircraft.

The issue was moot with respect to Delta 1989, for at 9:58, the ID Technicians announced to the floor that "1989 is no hijack, landing in Cleveland as a precautionary measure." The ID Technician called Boston Center at 9:59 and informed its military position:

At 10:03, the ID Technicians called Indianapolis Center and informed them that the Delta 1989 flight was not a hijack, but that they had four fighters scrambled on it "just to be sure" (fighters other than Otis and Langley). The Mission Crew Commander had scrambled fighters from Otis Air Force Base to respond to the situation in New York, and fighters from Langley to respond first to the reports of American 11 heading south, and then to establish a Combat Air Patrol over Washington, DC. These scrambles exhausted NEADS' complement of alert fighters. To intercept Delta 1989, the Mission Crew Commander scrambled fighters from Air National Guard units at Toledo, Ohio and Selfridge, Michigan.

At that moment, United 93, an aircraft about which the NEADS air defenders had heard absolutely nothing, crashed in Pennsylvania.

8.   UNITED 93

8.1 FAA Awareness

United Airlines Flight 93 began its takeoff roll from Newark International Airport at 8:42, some forty minutes late, and checked in with air traffic control at 8:43: "United 93 fourteen hundred [feet] for twenty-five hundred." All communications with Newark Tower, New York Tracon, and New York Air Route Traffic Center were normal; after reporting experiencing some "light chop" at 35,000 feet, the flight was handed off to Cleveland Center at 9:23. Several seconds later, United 93 established radio contact with

Cleveland Air Route Traffic Control Center: "Morning Cleveland, United Ninety-three with you at, three-five-oh (35,000 feet), intermittent light chop. The controller did not respond to this initial transmission as he had sixteen flights under his control, and was issuing new routes to several aircraft based upon the decisions in New York and Boston to ground—stop all aircraft.

United 93 again radioed Cleveland Center at 9:25, checking in at 35,000 feet. The controller replied, "United ninety-three, Cleveland, roger." The controller then engaged in conversation with several aircraft about the evolving situation in New York City and the prospects for flights to be allowed to land in Philadelphia; while the controller was extremely discreet, it was clear what he was talking about. The time was 9:26.

The controller, who was moving planes away from each other as the traffic built in his sector from the ground stop in New York and Boston, warned several planes, including United 93: "United 93 that traffic for you is one o'clock twelve miles eastbound three seven zero." The aircraft acknowledged: "Negative contact we're looking United Ninety-three." Then, at 9:28, the controller and the pilots of several other flights heard "a radio transmission of unintelligible sounds of possible screaming or a struggle from an unknown origin ..." The controller responded: "Somebody call Cleveland?" This was followed, at 9:29, by a second radio transmission, with sounds of screaming and someone yelling "Get out of here, get out of here," again from an unknown source. The Cleveland Center controllers began to try to identify the possible source of the transmissions, and noticed that United 93 had descended some 700 feet.

The controller responsible for United 93 attempted to contact the aircraft. There was no reply. The controller attempted again to raise United 93: "United ninety-three, verify three-five-zero (thirty-five thousand feet)." There was no reply. The controller tried to raise United 93 several more times, with no response. At 9:30, the controller began to poll the other flights on his frequency to determine the source of the noise.

At 9:32, a third radio transmission came over the frequency: "keep remaining sitting. We have a bomb on board."

Between 9:34 and 9:38, the controller observed United 93 climbing to forty thousand seven hundred feet. He moved several aircraft out of the way of the non-responsive United 93, including Delta 1989.

Pilots radioed in confirmation that they had heard that there was a bomb on board. The controller continued to try to contact United 93, and asked, at 9:36, whether the pilot could confirm that he had been hijacked. There was no response.

As the flight continued to climb and fly erratically, the controller moved decisively to clear the other flights in his sector from United 93's erratic flight path.

Then, at 9:39, another radio transmission came over the frequency from United 93.

When the flight did not respond, pilots on other flights confirmed that they had heard the transmission. The controller continued to move traffic out of the flight path of United 93 until, at 9:41, the center lost United 93's transponder signal:

The controller located the aircraft on primary radar, and matched his reading with visual sightings from other aircraft to follow the flight as it turned east and, ultimately, south.

While controllers at FAA's Cleveland Center tracked the path of United 93 as it headed east, it did not take long for Cleveland Center's managers to notify all levels of upper management of the grave situation developing on board United 93.

At approximately 9:39, Cleveland Center notified the Great Lakes Regional Operations Center in Chicago of the screams and statements relating to having a "bomb on board" that it believed were coming from United 93. Even before the region received notice of United 93, senior managers at both FAA headquarters and Command Center were notified of the report that United 93 had a bomb on board. Cleveland Center's notice to upper management was prompted by Command Center's request for information concerning suspicious aircraft. At approximately 9:18, the Deputy Director of Air Traffic at FAA headquarters established an open line of communication with a manager from the Command Center at Herndon. At approximately 9:25, FAA headquarters instructed Command Center to "get an awareness up to all the traffic management coordinators or the traffic management units to report any unusual circumstances direct to the Command Center of loss of identification, or any radio, uh, any unusual radio transmissions." At approximately 9:31, the National Traffic Management Officer on duty at Command Center executed the request from FAA Headquarters:

Approximately one minute after this request for information was sent to the FAA field facilities, Cleveland Center provided Command Center with the following urgent report:

In less than two minutes, at 9:34, Command Center relayed the information concerning United 93 to FAA Headquarters:

At approximately 9:36, Cleveland Center advised Command Center that they were still tracking United 93 and inquired specifically whether someone had requested the military to launch fighter aircraft to intercept United 93. Cleveland Center even told Command Center they were prepared to contact a nearby military base to request fighter aircraft assistance. Command Center told Cleveland Center that FAA personnel above them in the chain of command had to make the decision to request military assistance.

Indeed, from 9:34 to 10:08, a Command Center facility manager provided several updates to the Deputy Administrator and other executives at FAA headquarters as United 93 approached the Washington, DC area. Specifically, at 9:41, Command Center notified headquarters that United 93 had reversed course from its intended flight path and was descending:

At 9:42, Command Center learned through a television news report that a plane had struck the Pentagon. FAA headquarters also knew the Pentagon had been attacked by an aircraft. Shortly after Command Center heard about the crash at the Pentagon, Command Center's National Operations Manager, Ben Sliney, ordered all FAA facilities to instruct all airborne aircraft to land at the nearest airport. At the time the order was given, there were approximately 4,500 commercial and general aviation aircraft in the skies over the United States. All aircraft landed without incident. This was an unprecedented order. The air traffic control system handled it with great skill.

While Command Center employees informed FAA field facilities of the order to land all aircraft, one of the Command Center managers continued to give FAA headquarters several updates on the progress and location of United 93. In fact, at 9:46, 17 minutes before impact, Command Center gave this update on United 93 to FAA headquarters:

At 9:48, FAA Command Center told headquarters United 93 was on a course for Washington, DC:

At 9:49, Command Center suggest[ed] that someone at headquarters should decide whether to request military assistance:

[The timing of this conversation is consistent with the FAA Administrator Jane Garvey and her staff's having joined the Air Threat Conference Call run by Richard Clarke from the White House Situation Room. There is no evidence that the report passed to FAA Headquarters from the Command Center reached the military in a timely fashion.]

At 9:53, FAA headquarters informed Command Center that the Deputy Director for Air Traffic Services was talking to Deputy Administrator Monte Belger about scrambling aircraft. Then, at 9:56, Command Center informed headquarters they lost track of United 93 over the Pittsburgh area. Within seconds, Command Center located United 93 and informed headquarters:

At 10:00, Command Center advised headquarters that "United ninety three was spotted by a VFR at eight thousand feet, eleven, eleven miles south of Indianhead, just north of Cumberland, Maryland. At 10:01, just two minutes before United 93 crashed, Command Center provided FAA headquarters with the following update:

At 10:08, five minutes after United 93 crashed in a field in Pennsylvania, Command Center forwarded this update to headquarters:

At 10:17, Command Center advised headquarters of its belief that United 93 had "crashed fifteen miles south of Johnstown, Pennsylvania".

No one from FAA headquarters requested military assistance regarding United 93. In fact, the executive level managers at FAA headquarters did not forward the information they received from Command Center regarding United 93 to the military.

8.2 Military Notification and Response

NEADS first received a call about United 93 from the military liaison at Cleveland Center, at 10:07. This call was the first notification the military —at any level— received 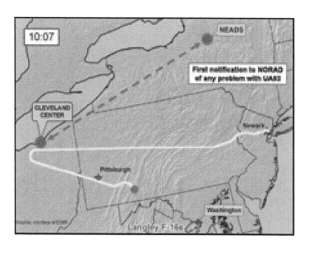 about United 93. Unaware that the aircraft had already crashed, Cleveland passed to NEADS the aircraft's last know latitude and longitude. NEADS was never able to locate United 93 on radar because it was already in the ground.

When the information that United 93 had turned off its transponder and had a potential bomb on board reached the mission crew commander, he was dealing with the arrival of the Langley fighters over Washington and what their orders were with respect to potential targets. While NEADS searched for the radar track on United 93, the Mission Crew Commander and his Weapons Director engaged in the following conversation shortly after 10:10 concerning the rules of engagement:

As the news of a bomb on board United 93 spread throughout the floor, the NEADS air defenders searched for the primary radar target and the Mission Crew Commander tried to locate assets to scramble toward the plane. At approximately 10:11, the commander got on the phone with an Air National Guard Unit in Syracuse:

NEADS Identification Technicians called Washington Center to provide a "heads up" to them about United 93, but Washington Center provided NEADS with startling new information on the flight:

The time was 10:15 and the call was NEADS' first notice that United 93 had crashed. The actual time of the crash was 10:03:11.

By 10:15, the NEADS air defenders knew that two aircraft had crashed into the World Trade Center, a third had crashed into the Pentagon, Delta 1989 had landed safely in Cleveland and was not a hijack, and United 93 had crashed in Pennsylvania.

The minutes after 10:15 were spent on the floor at NEADS attempting to mobilize other fighters from the eastern seaboard, and anticipating the arrival of Air Force Once in the Washington area. The Mission Crew Commander was notified at 10:25 that "Air Force One is airborne out of Florida heading to Washington. We've got those four F-15s coming out of Langley. They're done rolling. Two of them will be diverted to escort at the appropriate time."

Then, at 10:32, the MCC Technician read information that had just come across the Chat Log from CONR in Florida:

The NEADS air defenders have expressed considerable confusion over the nature and effect of this order in interviews with Commission staff. Indeed, Colonel Marr indicated to staff that he actually believes he withheld the order from the floor for several minutes because he was unsure of its ramification, while both the Mission Crew Commander and the Weapons Director indicated that they withheld the order from the pilots flying Combat Air Patrol over Washington, DC and New York City because they were unsure how the pilots would or should proceed with such an order. The Weapons Director [struggled with repeated requests from the pilots and controllers for clarification of the rules of engagement, but ultimately responded:]

The shoot-down [authorization] order was the first official "rules of engagement" (ROE) of the morning to come down through the chain of command at DOD to NEADS. At virtually the same time, the Department of Defense elevated its alert status to DEFCON 3. This alert posture was suited more to a Cold War conflict than to al Qaeda's attack. Nonetheless, the shift to an elevated alert status signified the reassertion of authority by the national command structure. The air defense of the United States — subsequently called operation "Noble Eagle" — had at last begun.

8.3 Commission Findings and Assessment

The operational facts of the military response to United 93, as reflected in the tapes and transcripts as corroborated by contemporaneous logs and witness interviews, contrast sharply with the official explanations of that response. The military did not receive notice that United 93 was a hijacking at 9:16, as reported to the Commission, in May 2003, by NORAD; that notice came at 10:07.

At 9:16, the MCC/T Log records: "United tail #N612UA/75 S0B/" This tail number corresponds not with United 93 but with United 175, which had crashed into the World Trade Center. A corresponding conversation on the subpoenaed tapes confirms that at 9:16 NEADS was receiving confirmation of the tail number of the United 175 flight.

Furthermore, at 9:16, the plane had not yet even been hijacked. In fact, the sounds of the initial struggle on board United 93 that resulted in its hijacking are not audible on the air traffic radio frequency in Cleveland Center until 9:28. As late as 9:25, moreover, according to FAA controller transcripts, the pilot of United 93 radioed in: "United ninety-three checking three- five-oh (35,000 feet)."

The "ground truth" revealed by the tapes, as corroborated by Commission staff, also belies the official version of the response to United 93 that is built on the early notification time. "Air War Over America," for instance, the 1st Air Force's official history of 9/11, offers the following accounts by two of the key NORAD participants:

(Colonel Robert Marr, NEADS Commander): "With all available alert fighters in the air, Marr and his crew were still faced with United Flight 93. The plane was headed west, so controllers began looking for any other fighter jets that might be nearby. We don't have fighters that way and we think he's headed toward Detroit or Chicago,' Marr says. `I'm thinking Chicago is the target and know that Selfridge Air National Guard Base (Mich.) has F-16s in the air. We contacted them so they could head 93 off at the pass. The idea is to get in there, close in on him and convince him to turn. As United Airlines Flight 93 was going out, we received the clearance to kill if need be. In fact, General Arnold's words almost verbatim were: `We will take lives in the air to save lives on the ground.'"

(General Larry Arnold, CONR Commander): "… we watched the 93 track as it meandered around the Ohio—Pennsylvania area and started to turn south toward DC. By now the Pentagon has been hit and we have aircraft on orbit . They are now orbiting over Washington, DC, and have been for a while. As United 93 headed toward DC, the desire is to move the fighters toward that aircraft."

The record demonstrates, however, that no-one at any level in NORAD (or DOD) ever "watched the 93 track" start to turn south toward DC. The only track that NEADS watched was the Delta 1989 track, which turned toward Cleveland. In fact, NORAD never saw United 93 at all. The Selfridge fighters were contacted not regarding United 93, but Delta 1989. Most important, NORAD certainly never "received the clearance to kill if need be" on United 93;

indeed, as determined by Commission staff, as late as 10:10 the ROE orders given by the NEADS Mission Crew Commander were "negative clearance to shoot" regarding targets over Washington, DC.

9.   THE IMPACT OF INACCURATE STATEMENTS

Any attempt to assess the performance of the FAA and NORAD in responding to the hijackings on 9/11 must distinguish between the operational actions of that day and the government's descriptions of those actions in the days, months, and years that have followed. Ironically, the sequence of FAA notifications and NORAD responses presented to the Commission—in which the military had 47 minutes' notice on United 93 and 14 minutes' notice on American 77—raised questions about the adequacy of the military's response that were unnecessary given the actual notice to the military on those flights (zero advance notice on either flight).

We do not believe that understanding the truth about the events of that morning reflects discredit on the operational personnel from NEADS or FAA facilities. The NEADS commanders and floor officers actively reached out in seeking information, and made the best judgments they could based on the information they possessed. Individual FAA controllers, facility managers, and Command Center managers thought outside the box in recommending a nationwide alert, in ground—stopping local traffic, and, ultimately, in deciding to land all aircraft and executing that unprecedented order flawlessly.

But we have reached these conclusions about the operational facts of the day in spite of the government's version of those events, not because of it. In assessing the agencies' performance on 9/11, Commission staff has had to contend with four fundamentally inaccurate representations of fact by the government: (1) that notice was received of United 93 at 9:16; (2) that notice was received of American 77 at 9:24; (3) that the Langley fighters were scrambled to meet the threats posed by United 93 and/or American 77; and (4) that the military was following United 93 and in position to shoot the flight down if it approached Washington, DC. Although our focus has been on establishing the operational facts, and not on establishing the source of the inaccurate testimony, our research has revealed that the inaccurate statements have a tortuous history.

Inaccurate Statement 1: The FAA notified the military at 9:16 that United 93 was hijacked.

This inaccurate statement can be traced to the week after 9/11. NORAD's first publicly available timeline of the events of 9/11 was released on September 18, 2001, one week after the attacks. Prior to the September 18th release, NORAD Public Affairs prepared a draft release, dated September 16th. The draft release listed the time 9:16 as the notification time for United 93.

Between the September 16th draft and the September 18th final release, that time was changed. In the final release, the 9:16 notification time for United 93 is deleted, and is replaced with "N/A." The release explains that the notification time is "N/A" because the FAA informed NORAD of the hijacking of United 93 while on an open line discussing American 77. The NORAD Public Affairs Director stated to Commission staff that he deleted the 9:16 notification time because he "lost confidence" in its accuracy, although he could not remember why he lost confidence in the time.

An email obtained the Commission in response to the Commission's NORAD subpoena sheds some light on why NORAD may have lost confidence in the 9:16 notification time. The e-mail, sent on September 16, 2001 at 11:06 p.m. to NEADS from Brigadier General Doug Moore at CONR, commends the person at NEADS "who dug up the requested information from your logs and tapes," and indicates that it has been passed to "the proper FAA office" which will be "using this data to brief the White House tomorrow" [i.e., September 17]. The e-mail then asks for follow-up information about, among other data points, "United 93, 1408Z [i.e., 10:08], which center calls with information that United 93 ... is heading for Cleveland? ... 1415Z [i.e., 10:15], who reported to NEADS that aircraft had crashed?"

This e-mail – and the response to it by NEADS – is significant because it reveals that someone at NEADS had searched the relevant logs and tapes during the first week after 9/11 and identified the time at which the FAA notified NEADS about United 93. It is a fair inference that, having identified the notification time, NORAD "lost confidence" in 9:16 and omitted it from the September 18 release.

The question, then, is why the discredited 9:16 notification time reappeared in NORAD's testimony before the Commission. This question becomes more perplexing when one considers the testimony of Cherie Gott, a data analyst at NORAD headquarters, in a Commission interview. Ms. Gott related that a timeline she created based on the September 18th press release (which reflected no notification time for United 93) was forwarded to

NORAD officials at CONR on May 13, 2003 — a week prior
to the Commission's hearing — in order to prepare CONR
officials for their testimony.
Why was 9:16 reintroduced? The Commission has
obtained an e-mail sent from Col. Marr to retired Col.
Scott (who worked at CONR) after the Commission's
hearing, which sheds light on the subject. During the May
hearing, Commissioner Lehman asked several questions
about the flight path of the Langley fighters, who traveled
directly east, over the ocean, and then north toward
Baltimore, before heading west to Washington. Why, the
Commissioner wanted to know, didn't the fighters head
more directly to Washington, if they had been scrambled
to respond to American 77, the plane that struck the
Pentagon? Col. Marr addressed this question in his e-mail
response to retired Col. Scott:

"The answer on AA77 is not easy, nor is it pretty.
At the time AA77 was occurring we were focused
on UAL93 which was the only confirmed hijack
that the FAA had identified to us. My records
show UAL93 reported as hijacked at 0916L, once
we found it and identified it's [sic] westerly
heading, we scrambled Langley at 0924L just in
case it turned around toward DC, which it did
later. At 0924L we also received a call from the
FAA about AA77 with a follow-up call at 0925L.
It is easiest to explain the simultaneous scramble
order with the AA77 notification as the scramble
being against AA77 — it takes a lot of time to
explain to the public that you're scrambling
fighters against a plane heading away from the
possible target."

Col. Marr, in other words, attempts to explain the circuitous route of the Langley fighters in getting to Washington, DC by indicating that they were not in fact scrambled to respond to a report at 9:24 that American 77 was hijacked; they were scrambled in response to the earlier "report" that United 93 was hijacked. Thus, the reintroduction of the discredited 9:16 notification time enabled NORAD to explain to the Commission the odd route of the Langley fighters in reaching Washington.

There were two fundamental problems with the explanation. First, as at least some in the military have known since the week of 9/11, it is inaccurate. United 93 had not been hijacked at 9:16; the hijacking did not occur until 9:28 — after the Langley fighters were ordered scrambled — and NEADS was not notified until after the plane had crashed. NORAD informed Commission staff at the close of interviews at Colorado Springs (and again publicly at the Commission's hearing in June 2004) that it now accepts that notification did not occur until after the plane had crashed. Second, as we will now discuss, NEADS was not notified that American 77 was hijacked at 9:24.

Inaccurate Statement 2: The FAA notified the military of the hijacking of American 77 at 9:24.

Although American 77 disappeared from radar and radio at 8:56, the first notification to NEADS that American 77 was missing (there is no mention of its having been hijacked at this point) came at 9:34, ten minutes after the scramble had already been ordered at Langley Air Force Base.

One to two minutes later, NEADS received notice that an unidentified plane was six miles southwest of the White House. American 77 crashed into the Pentagon at 9:37:45.

Thus, NEADS did not receive notice that American 77 was hijacked at 9:24. In fact, NEADS never received notice that American 77 was hijacked at all, let alone at 9:24; it received reports (at 9:34) that American 77 was missing, and (at 9:35 or 9:36) that an unidentified plane was near the White House.

What notification did occur at 9:24? The Mission Crew Commander's staff at NEADS maintains a handwritten contemporaneous log of information received and actions taken (known as the "MCC/T Log"). The 9/11 entry in the log at 9:24 records: "American Airlines #N334AA hijacked." This tail number refers not to American 77 but to American 11, the first hijacked aircraft that crashed into the North Tower of the World Trade Center. The subpoenaed tapes confirm that this time corresponds to NEADS's receipt of tail number information on American 11 and to reports that American 11 was still airborne and headed towards Washington, DC.

Inaccurate Statement 3: The Langley fighters were scrambled in response to the FAA's notification to the military, at 9:24, that American 77 was hijacked.

Contrary to testimony before the Commission, the Langley fighters were ordered scrambled not because of United 93, which had not been hijacked, nor because of American 77, which had not yet been reported to NEADS, but because of the mistaken report that American 11 — the first hijacked plane — had not hit the World Trade

Center, but was heading south towards Washington, DC. The fighters were ordered scrambled initially toward New York, and then vectored toward Baltimore, in an effort to intercept that mistakenly reported aircraft. The best evidence for both this false report and the resulting scramble is the subpoenaed NEADS tape, which records that at approximately 9:21, the Mission Crew Commander spoke the following to the Battle Cab (where the Battle Commander, Colonel Marr, was located):

> "Okay. American Airlines is still airborne, 11, the first guy. He's headed towards Washington, okay? I think we need to scramble Langley right now, and I'm going to—I'm going to take the fighters from Otis and try to chase this guy down if I can find him. Yeah. You sure? Okay. He's heading towards Langley, or I should say Washington. American 11, the original guy. He's still airborne…"

Seconds later, the Mission Crew Commander ordered the scramble of the Langley fighters.

This report of American 11 heading south – the cause of the Langley scramble—is reflected not just in taped conversations at NEADS, but in taped conversations at FAA centers, on chat logs compiled at NEADS, CONR, NORAD, and the National Military Command Center, and in other records. It is the opening report on the national level, multi-agency "Significant Event Conference" call. The mistaken report was also readily acknowledged in interviews of NORAD's operational personnel who participated in the 9/11 response.

But in October 2001, for instance, NORAD Commanding General Ralph Eberhart testified before the Senate
Armed Services Committee on the sequence of events
on 9/11. General Eberhart did not mention the mistaken
report about American 11 as a cause for the `Langley
scramble. Instead, he provided a timeline chart and verbal
testimony that listed 9:24 as the notification time for
American 77 and implied that this notification prompted
the scramble of the Langley fighters.

The General elaborated, in responses submitted after
his testimony for the record: "The FAA notified the NEADS
that American Airlines Flight 77 was headed towards
Washington, DC. NEADS then passed this information
to NORAD's Air Warning Center .... At 0925, the NMCC
convened a Significant Event Conference and during that
conference, at 0933, NORAD reported one more aircraft
en route to Washington, DC."

NORAD's own Headquarters Intel Chat Log belies
this testimony, recording at 9:24:39 "original aa flt hijack is
now headed to Washington scrambled lfi,[i.e., Langley]"
and then at 9:25:13 "2 acrft that hit wt bldg not repeat not
the original hjk aa acrft." Furthermore, the Air Warning
Center log at NORAD, to which General Eberhart refers,
records, at 9:27, that "The original hijack a/c is still a/b and
head for Washington, DC Otis F15 are trying to intercept
the flight." It then records, at 9:36, that CONR has advised
of the scramble at Langley: "LFI A/B Quit 25/26/27 3
A/B at time 1333 [i.e., 9:33]." The NORAD Headquarters
chat log states, at 9:28: "R[eal] W[orld] Hijacking (original
notification) assessed by Intel as headed to Washington,
DC/2XF-15s in tail chase." [NCT 0005098].

General Eberhart's submission for the record, moreover, that NORAD reported "one more aircraft en route to Washington, DC" on the Significant Event Conference at 9:33 may have been literally true. Consistent, however, with NORAD's own records and the transcript of the Conference, the aircraft that NORAD reported to the Conference was not American 77, as the submission for the record implied, but American 11.

General Eberhart's responses to the Senate Armed Services Committee's "Questions for the Record" were not extemporaneous answers.

Inaccurate Statement 4: Military officials were tracking United 93 and intended to intercept the aircraft if it continued towards Washington, DC.

At the Commission's hearing in May 2003, Vice Chairman Hamilton expressed concern that the detailed timeline presented by NORAD omitted a significant time sequence: when the shoot-down authorization was passed from the President through the chain of command to the pilots. General Arnold backed away from the claim that the order was received prior to the crash of United 93, indicating his belief that it had been received a few minutes later. Because the NORAD witnesses had testified that they had been tracking United 93 for some forty-five minutes when it crashed, however, General Arnold was able to state with assurance that the flight would have been intercepted prior to reaching Washington, DC.

The issue of whether the military had been tracking United 93, and was therefore in position to intercept the flight if it approached Washington, DC, arose within days of the 9/11 attacks. On September 15, 2001, General Paul Weaver, overall commander of the Air National Guard which provided the fighters used to scramble Otis and Langley, told reporters that no fighters were scrambled or vectored to chase United 93: "There was no notification for us to launch airplanes. We weren't even close."

That same day, however, Deputy Secretary Wolfowitz stated in a television interview that Defense Department officials had been "following" United 93 and were prepared to shoot it down if it approached Washington, DC.

Officials have been steadfast since in stating that the military had been tracking United 93 and were in position to intercept and, if necessary, shoot down the flight. Notably, Col. Marr states in the U.S. Air Force's official history of 9/11, Air War Over America: "As United Airlines Flight 93 was going out [west toward Chicago], we received the clearance to kill if need be." Similarly, on an ABC News Special marking the one-year anniversary of 9/11, Col. Marr made inaccurate statements about the interception of United 93.

NORAD now acknowledges that at all levels — NEADS, CONR, and NORAD headquarters — they were completely unaware of United 93 as it was "going out" toward the west. Indeed, NEADS never learned of the flight until five minutes after it had crashed. NEADS never followed or was able to find the flight on radar, and was in fact still searching for the flight at 10:15, when the MCC/T Log and the subpoenaed tapes record FAA notification that the flight had crashed.

Furthermore, NORAD did not receive any form of shoot-down authority until 10:31. Even then, that instruction was not communicated to the pilots. Eventually, there were Air National Guard pilots over Washington with rules of engagement allowing them to engage. But they had received their direction outside of the usual military chain of command and did not get into the skies over Washington until after 10:40. In short, the representation that military had been following United 93 as it progressed, and was by virtue of this awareness in position to intercept the plane, was inaccurate.

10. CONCLUSION

The primary source material from 9/11 — the contemporaneous logs, other records, and tapes obtained by the Commission largely through subpoena and set forth at length in this monograph — reveal a sequence of events that had never been made public prior to the Commission's June 17, 2004 hearing. That sequence reveals that the military received hijack notification on American 11 nine minutes prior to its crash, and no hijack notification on any of the other flights prior to their crashes. The FAA's failure to notify NORAD or NEADS on United 175 is explained by its preoccupation with American 11; its failure to notify NORAD or NEADS on American 77 is explained by its loss of radar and radio contact with the aircraft. More difficult to understand is the failure to notify the military or request assistance on United 93, when FAA headquarters knew about the hijacking within six minutes of its occurrence and twenty-nine minutes prior to its crash. See Summary Tables.

At 10:02 that morning, [with one of the Trade Center Towers having collapsed and the other in flames, with the Pentagon burning and confusion reigning at the highest levels of government and command, and with a desperate struggle taking place, unbeknownst to the military, in the skies over Pennsylvania,] an officer on the floor at NEADS was recorded observing, "This is a new type of war."

He was right. America's air defense system was unprepared for the 9/11 attacks. FAA controllers and managers and the NEADS air defenders struggled, under difficult circumstances, to improvise a homeland defense against an unprecedented challenge they had never encountered and had never trained to meet.

[At the end of the day, however, although the decisions they had made that morning ran counter to the existing training and rules, and were made under the most intense pressure, the NORAD air defenders were well aware of the historical significance of those decisions. Prepared or not, they had ushered all of us into a new era.]

SUMMARY TABLES

Table 1: Hijack Times and FAA Awareness of Hijack

		Hijack Time*	FAA Awareness of Hijack	
Flight	Impact	Time	Time	Time Lapse
AA11	8:46:40	8:14-8:20	8:25	5-11 minutes
UA175	9:03:02	8:42-8:46	8:55	9-13 minutes
AA77	9:37:46	8:54-8:56	9:24**	28-30 minutes
UA93	10:03:11	9:28	9:28	0 minutes

* Estimated Hijacking Times

** Between 8:56 and 9:09, the relevant FAA Center believed AA77 had crashed. Between 9:09 and 9:21, based on the events in New York, information from American Airlines and the inability to confirm the crash on the ground, the FAA began to believe that AA77 might also be hijacked. By 9:24 the belief that AA77 may have been hijacked was communicated to FAA headquarters.

Table 2: FAA Awareness of Hijack and FAA Warning to the Military

Flight	Impact	FAA Awareness of Hijack Time	Notification to the Military Time	Time Lapse
AA11	8:46:40	8:25	8:38	13 minutes
UA175	9:03:02	8:55	9:03	8 minutes
AA77	9:37:46	9:24**	None	———
UA93	10:03:11	9:28	10:07	39 minutes

** Between 8:56 and 9:09, the relevant FAA Center believed AA77 had crashed. Between 9:09 and 9:21, based on the events in New York, information from American Airlines and the inability to confirm the crash on the ground, the FAA began to believe that AA77 might also be hijacked. By 9:24 the belief that AA77 may have been hijacked was communicated to FAA headquarters.

Table 3: FAA Warning to the Military

Flight	Impact	Notification as established by Commission Staff Time	Warning	Notification presented by NORAD to the Commission at May 2003 Hearing Time	Warning
AA11	8:46:40	8:38	9 minutes	8:40	7 minutes
UA175	9:03:02	9:03	0 minutes	9:05	0 minutes
AA77	9:37:46	None *	0 minutes	9:24	14 minutes
UA93	10:03:11	10:07	0 minutes	9:16	47 minutes

* There was no notification received by NEADS that American 77 was hijacked. Washington Center informed NEADS at 9:34 that American 77 was lost in Indianapolis Center's airspace and could not be found. This notification was separate from and preceded the information NEADS received at 9:36 from Boston Center that there was an "aircraft VFR six miles southeast of the White House... six southwest." NEADS did not know that aircraft, which struck the Pentagon a minute later, was American 77.

260

Glossary

AFIO	Agreement for Fighter Interceptor Operations
Air Force One	Presidential Plane with the President aboard
Al-Qaeda	Global militant Islamist Organization founded by Osama bin Laden in Peshawar, Afghanistan, in 1988/1989
AFB	Air Force Base
ARB	Air Reserve Base
(the) Battery	Southern tip of Manhattan Island
Boatlift	Normally the practice of lifting a boat out of the water for repairs or storage — On 9/11, it was taken to mean removing survivors by boat
CIA	Central Intelligence Agency
DIA	Defense Intelligence Agency
EMS	Emergency Medical Services
EMT	Emergency Medical Technician
F-15 Eagle	Twin-engine, all-weather tactical fighter providing air superiority in combat and homeland defense
FAA	Federal Aviation Administration
FBI	Federal Bureau of Investigation
FEMA	Federal Emergency Management Agency
Ground Zero	Impact zone of a nuclear device; in this case, the planes of 9/11
KSM	Khalid Sheihk Mohammed

NCA	National Command Authority — Establishes protocols for legal issuance of launch orders. Only the President or Secretary of Defense or their duly deputized successors, are the ultimate lawful source of military orders
NCTC	National Counterterrorism Center
NEADS	Northeast Air Defense Sector
NID	National Intelligence Department, aka National Institute of Defense, sometimes used for National Intelligence Director
NIST	National Institue of Standards and Technology
NORAD	North American Aerospace Defense Command
N/E Corridor	Area of land and air connecting Washington, New York and Boston
NSA	National Security Agency
NYFD	New York Fire Department
NYPD	New York Police Department
Otis Air Base	Otis Air National Guard Base; also referred to as Otis Air Force Base
PATH	Underground commuter trains running between the WTC and New Jersey
P.T.S.D.	Post Traumatic Stress Syndrome
Transponder	Electronic device that produces a response when it receives a radio-response interrogation that helps in identifying an aircraft's location
USNS	United States Navy Sealift
WTC	World Trade Center

References and Suggested Reading

_____. *Above Hallowed Ground: A Photographic Record of September 11, 2001*, New York: The Penguin Group

Ambinder, Marc. "Airport Security: Where the New Normal Has Become (Almost) Routine." *New York Magazine*, August 27, 2011, p. 36. <nymag.com/news/9-11/10th-anniversary/ airport/security>

Baldwin, Carly. "Seismic Impact of WTC Collapse. *Metro*, February 15, 2011, pp. 1-2. <www.metro.us/newyork/local/article/774044-seismic-impact-of-wtc-collapse>

Bate, Allison. "Armada Rescues Trapped New Yorkers," *Marine Digest*, October, 2001.

Benson, Eric. "The Planes: Flying Weapons." *New York Magazine*, August 27, 2011, p. 1. <nymag.com/ news/9-11/10th-anniversary/planes>

Bergen, Peter. *The Osama bin Laden I Know: An Oral History of al Qaeda's Leader* (2nd Ed). New York: Free Press, 2006.

Bickman, Jed and Walter Armstrong. "Alcoholism, Addiction & September 11th." Wikipedia, the Free Encyclopedia, September 9, 2011. <www.the fix.com/content/911-and-addiction-10-years-later8010?page_all>

Clarke, Richard A. *Against All Enemies, Inside American War on Terror.* New York: The Free Press, a division of Simon & Schuster, Inc., 2004.

de Vries, Karen, "9/11: Scrambled F-15's from Otis Air Force Base: Mach 1.5 or Cruise Speed?" Global Research, October 4, 2004, pp. 1-3. <http://globalresearch.ca/articles/VR1410A.html>

Dumas, Charlotte. *Retrieved,* Los Angeles: The Ice Plant, October 15, 2011.

G., Vincent. "How Fast Can An F-14, F-15, F-16, and F-22 Really Go?" *Yahoo Answers*, July 14, 2010. <http://answers.yahoo.com/question/index?qid=2010071435837AAHNjNx>

Giles, Matthew. "Total Progressive Collapse: Why, Precisely, the Towers Fell." *New York Magazine,* August 27, 2011, p. 128. <nymag.com/news/9-11/10th-anniversary/towers-collapse>

Helvarg, David. *Rescue Warriors: the U.S. Coast Guard, America's Forgotten Heroes,* Thomas Dunne Books: First Edition (May 12, 2009). New York: St. Martin's Press.

Herrup, Katharine. "Boatlifters: The Unknown Story of 9/11," Reuters, September 9, 2011. <http://blogs.reuters.com/katharine-herrup/2011/ 09/09/boatlifters-the-unknown-story-of-911>

Kolker, Robert. "Stairwell A: The Only Way Out," *New York Magazine*, August 27, 2011. <nymag.com/news/9-11/10th-anniversary/stairwell-a>

Lebwohl, Beth. "Pieces of Demolished World Trade Center Aboard Mars Rovers." September 10, 2011. <EarthSky.org/human-world/pieces-of-demolished-world-trade-center-aboard-mars-rovers>

Linfield, Susie. "Jumpers: Why the most haunting images of 2001 were hardly ever seen." *New York Magazine*, August 27, 2011, p. 82. <nymag.com/news/9/11/10th-anniversary/jumpers>

McDougall, Christopher. "Reasons They Haven't Hit Us Again." *New York,* May 21,2005, p. 124. <nymag.com/nymetro/news/features/10560/>

Patrick, Meghan. MSC Public Affairs. "CIVMARs remember 9/11, *Sealift*—U.S. Navy's Newsletter (Military Sealift Command), October, 2011. <www.msc.navy.mil/sealift/2011/October/remember.htm>
Rich, Frank. "Day's End: The 9/11 decade is now over. The terrorists lost but who won?" *New York Magazine*, August 27,2011, pp. 27–30. <nymag.com/news/9-11/10th_anniversary/frank-rich>

Saulman, Greg. "9/11 10th Anniversary: F-15 Pilot Dan Nash Recalls Response," *The Republican*, September 5, 2011, pp. 1-6. <http://connect.masslive.com/gsaulman/index.html>

Sherman, Jake. "Pence Likens Health Care Ruling to
    9/11." *Politico,* June 28, 2012, p. 1.
    <www.politico.com/blogs/on-congress/2012/
    pence-likens-health-care-ruling-to-127628.html>

Smith, Dennis. *Report from Ground Zero.* New York:
    Plume, a member of Penguin Putnam, Inc., February
    25, 2003.

Spencer, Lynn. *Touching History: The Untold Story of the
    Drama That Unfolded in the Skies Over America on
    9/11.* New York: The Free Press, a Division of Simon
    & Schuster, June 2008.

Spilman, Rick. "Maritime Evacuation on 9/11 – An
    American Dunkirk," *The Old Salt Blog,* September
    11, 2009.
    <www.oldsaltblog.com/2009/09/11-maritime-
    evacuation-on-911-an-american-dunkirk/>

Taylor, Rob. "Afghan Taliban says rehearsed attack
    for two months." *Reuters,* April 15, 2012. <www.
    reuters.com/article/2012/04/16/us-afghan-taliban-
    plan-idUSBRE83FOLX20210416>

United States v. Usama bin Laden et al. S(7) 98Cr1023.
    Testimony of Jamal Ahmed Mohammed al-Fadl
    (S.N.N.Y., February 6, 2001), Transcript for Day 2
    of the Trial, 6 February 2001.

Unknown author. "Paper, Dispersal of," *New York Magazine*, August 27, 2011, p. 100. <nymag.com/news/9-11/10th-anniversary/paper/>

Weaver, Mary Anne. "Lost at Tora Bora." *New York Times Magazine*, December 16, 2001, p. 54. <www.nytimes.com/2005/09/11magazine?11TORABORA.html?>

Wikipedia, the Free Encyclopedia. "Al Qaeda." <http://en.wikipedia.org/wiki/Al-Qaeda>

Wikipedia, the Free Encyclopedia. "Casualties of the September 11 Attacks." <http://en.wikipedia.org/Casualties_of_the_September_11_attacks>

Wikipedia, the Free Encyclopedia. "Collapse of the World Trade Center." <http://en.wikipedia.org/wiki/Collapse_of_the_World_Trade_Center_>

Wikipedia, the Free Encyclopedia. "Eastern Air Defense Sector." <http://en.wikipedia.org/wiki/Rsdyrtm_Defense_Sector>

Wikipedia, the Free Encyclopedia. "Federal Bureau of Investigation." <http://en.wikipedia.org/wiki/Federal_Bureau_Air_of_Investigation>

Wikipedia, the Free Encyclopedia. "Hijackers in the
     September 11 attacks." <http://en.wikipedia.org/
     wiki_Hijackers_in_the_September_11_attacks>

Wikipedia, the Free Encyclopedia. "How many people
     died in the September 11 attacks." <http://
     en.wikipedia.org/wiki_answers.com/Q/How_
     many_people_died_in_the_September_11_attacks>

Wikipedia, the Free Encyclopedia. "National Command
     Authority."
     <http://en.wikipedia.org/wiki/National_
     Command_Authority,April24,2012>

Wikipedia, the Free Encyclopedia. "Taliban, Participant
     in the Civil War in Afghanistan, the War in
     Afghanistan (2001-Present)."
     <http://en.wikipedia.org/wiki/Taliban>

Wikipedia, the Free Encyclopedia. "Timeline of the
     September 11 attacks."
     <http://en.wikipedia.org/wiki/timeline_for_the_
     Day_of_the_September_11_attacks>
Wikipedia, the Free Encyclopedia. "Transponder
     (aviation)." <http://en.wikipedia.org/wiki/
     Transponder_(aviation)>

Wikipedia, the Free Encyclopedia. "USNS Comfort
     (Y-AH-20): Main article: Operation Noble Eagle
     — USNS Comfort Hospital ship activated the
     afternoon of September 11th arriving at Pier 92 in

Manhattan on September 14 to treat rescue workers in the clinic aboard ship. <http://en,wikipedia.org/wiki/USNS_Comfort_ (T-AH20)_Operation_Noble_Eagle>

Wikipedia, the Free Encyclopedia. "United States Secret Service." <http://en.wikipedia.org/wiki/United_ States_Secret_Service>

Wikipedia, the Free Encyclopedia. "USS *New York* (LPD-21)." <http://en.wikipedia.org/wiki/USS_ NewYork_(LPD-21)>

Wikipedia, the Free Encyclopedia. "WTC Building Arrangement and Site Plan.svg." <http://en.wikipedia.org/wiki/File:WTC_ Building_Arrangement_and_Site_Plan.svg>

Zengerle, Jason. "Homeland Security: Big threats, bigger government." *New York Magazine,* August 27, 2011, p. 75. <nymag.com/news/9-11/10th-anniversary/ homeland-security/>

About the Author

Bert Upson (Adman – Educator – Adventurer – Lecturer – Writer), is a business leader with many vital life experiences in the fields of sales, marketing, advertising, teaching and now, writing his first book.

In the advertising agency business he led in the creation of breakthrough campaigns for national consumer brands, winning awards of two Clios for "Excellence in Television Advertising" and an Effie for "Proven Ability of Corporate Advertising to Sell Product."

His most noteworthy accomplishment was in the paper industry as general manager at the American Paper Institute where he became known as a national advocate of housewives saving old newspapers for recycling into consumer and industrial packaging. This became known as "Save the Trees." It was a major conservation movement under Bert's tutelage. In his farewell address, after substantial growth in the industry, he received the industry's highest honor, election to the Packaging Education Foundation's Hall of Fame, and a standing ovation from paper industry leaders.

As president of his own private firm since 1992, CEO, Inc., he has counseled several hundred executives of Fortune 500 companies in improving their management and leadership skills and implementing culture change throughout the organization.

As a consultant, Bert has authored several leadership training manuals, including "Goal Works" and "Senior Moments" which were the foundation of his management leadership development seminars throughout the United States.

Upson earned his degree from Yale University in 1955 with honors as a European History major and, later, became certified as a master facilitator of the world-renowned "Investment In Excellence" personal leadership program of the Pacific Institute in Seattle, Washington.

Bert is well-traveled. As a younger man he ventured into the jungles of Venezuela as a drilling assistant on an iron ore exploration project, traveled on tramp steamers in the Caribbean, visited every state in the union; and since his marriage to his wife, Joan, in 1985, he has been fortunate in traversing the Panama Canal, sailing throughout the Western Pacific and touring all European nations.

He has served his community as lieutenant of the Citizens on Patrol under the Riverside Sheriff's Department and as director of the Homeowner's Association of the Shadow Mountain Resort. He was a Big Brother, is a director of the Stanford Club of the Desert and a member of the Palm Springs Chapter of the Retired Officers Association of America.

Bert is now creating a special lecture series designed to inform and educate students and civic groups about the facts and the historical implications of 9/11 on American society and values.

Bert Upson

Prayer for September 11

Good Shepherd, please watch over those who suffer,
Those who have been hurt in one way or another,
Those who have lost someone dear,
Those who are hurting year after year.
May those souls and the ones who have died
Be blessed and comforted in your loving light.
Amen.

—Janet Asten,
Rancho Mirage, California

Made in the USA
San Bernardino, CA
18 August 2013